Guizot de Witt

A Parisian Family

Guizot de Witt

A Parisian Family

ISBN/EAN: 9783743310964

Manufactured in Europe, USA, Canada, Australia, Japa

Cover: Foto ©ninafisch / pixelio.de

Manufactured and distributed by brebook publishing software (www.brebook.com)

Guizot de Witt

A Parisian Family

'Mamma! mamma! why did you not send for me?'

Frontispiece. Page 9.

A Parisian Family

TRANSLATED FROM THE FRENCH OF

MADAME GUIZOT DE WITT

BY THE

AUTHOR OF 'JOHN HALIFAX, GENTLEMAN'

FOR

Girls in their Teens

LONDON
SAMPSON LOW, SON, AND MARSTON
CROWN BUILDINGS, 188 FLEET STREET
1871

Contents.

CHAPTER		PAGE
I	DEATH IN THE HOUSE	1
II	MOTHERLESS	12
III	THE ELDEST SISTER	23
IV	IN THE COUNTRY	33
V	THE CHRISTENING	45
VI	PARIS ONCE MORE	56
VII	AT THE TUILERIES	67
VIII	GOING SHOPPING	79
IX	THE BOYS AT SCHOOL	89
X	THE GIRLS AND THEIR FRIENDS	101
XI	A LEARNED MAN'S DAUGHTER	114

CONTENTS.

CHAPTER		PAGE
XII	SUMMER-TIME	129
XIII	THE PLEASURE-PARTY	144
XIV	A GRAND IDEA	157
XV	AT BRESSUIRE	172
XVI	COUNTRY COUSINS	185
XVII	IN THE PARIS WORLD	198
XVIII	DIFFICULTIES RISE	210
XIX	DEBTS AND DANGER	222
XX	THE CRISIS	236
XXI	A LONG JOURNEY	251
XXII	THE CATASTROPHE	263
XXIII	ANGUISH	277
XXIV	SICKNESS UNTO DEATH	289
XXV	DEATH PASSES BY	302
XXVI	A NEW CAREER	314
XXVII	HOME AT LAST	327

A Parisian Family.

CHAPTER I.

DEATH IN THE HOUSE.

'NO, no, husband,' said Madame Rambert in a feeble voice: 'I do not wish you to send for Louise; she is so well amused, poor child, and I need nobody.'

'Nevertheless, it seems to me that Louise's place is beside her sick mother,' replied M. Rambert.

'Not at all; she will have plenty of sorrow in her life. I would rather keep her happy as long as is possible.'

M. Rambert stifled a sigh, and consented to his wife's wish. It did not occur to him to consider whether it was well thus to hide completely from children the dark side of life. He was a busy man; he had never interfered in the education of his girls, and his only boy, Arthur, was at college. Louise, therefore, was left in the country, where she had been staying with one of her aunts, gathering violets and periwinkles, running in the wood that was fast covering itself in its summer dress of tender green, laughing all day long with her cousins, and never once troubling herself about Paris and her parents. 'What news of your mother?' her aunt would ask when the postman came, but often Louise had no letter at all, and when one came she generally answered carelessly, 'Oh! mamma is not quite well; you know, aunt, she always suffers more or less,' and then skipped away to hunt after butterflies.

In spite of her sixteen years, Louise was still extremely childish. Her mother had endured uncomplainingly years of feeble health, and, by force of courage ill applied, had succeeded in doing all her duties as mother and mistress, in order that no cares might fall upon her daughter. Yet Louise was the eldest of four—Arthur, aged fourteen; Anna, twelve; Caroline, ten. The difference was great between herself and her sisters: and though she still continued lessons, she had already began to see a little of society, and to visit with her young companions. 'Why torment and disquiet the child before her time comes?' Madame Rambert would say whenever a friend came in and found the sick mother alone.

Alas! the time of sorrow came at length, without forewarning. Louise, descending one morning, fresh as a rose and gay as spring, found her aunt in tears.

'What is the matter?' cried she, darting to the sofa. 'Has the postman brought you ill news? Nobody carried the letters up to my room to-day.'

The poor child began to weep also. Her aunt took her in her arms silently; then with an effort she said, 'Louise, your mother is worse; your father has sent for you home.'

'Màmma worse! Oh! quick, quick, aunt! put to the horses. I will pack my trunk in a minute. I want nobody; I can go to Paris alone.'

'Your uncle is going with you, my child.'

This single idea struck terror into the heart of Louise. What! her uncle—so busy that he could not go out for a walk—always buried in his books—who had even left Paris with the excuse that the noise of the streets worried him in his work—her uncle was going to quit his study, and lose an entire day in taking her home? He must then be very uneasy.

Still weeping, Madame de Bresse assisted her niece to fold up her dresses, collect her books, handkerchiefs, ribbons, which were tossing about on all sides. She had just turned the key of the trunk, and given it to Louise, telling her not to lose it, when the carriage drove up to the door.

'Good-bye, aunt! good-bye, Marie and Joanne!' cried the young girl, whom the excitement of departure had already made less sad. 'I will write to-morrow, and tell you all about mamma. I hope to find her better; she is so often ill, and it all passes away.'

But Madame de Bresse embraced her niece mournfully. She had less hope in her sister's illness passing away. 'If you need me I will come at once,' she whispered as she put Louise into the carriage. What! her aunt, who never could be persuaded to leave home and children? Louise's alarm increased more and more.

The journey from Bressuire to Coulomniers was a silent one. M. de Bresse was not accustomed to talk much with children. Besides, he disapproved entirely of Louise's having been kept in ignorance of her mother's danger. He would have forewarned her of it himself, but knew not how: he detested tears and 'scenes.' They reached Coulomniers, entered the railway-carriage, the stations were disappearing one after the other, and still M. de Bresse had only spoken to his niece to ask her if she would like the window shut or open.

Paris was near; the little scattered villas grew into streets; and Louise, reassured by her uncle's silence, began to watch the houses gliding by, and to wonder vaguely how many people lived in these small dwellings, which often consisted only of one story, with two windows in the roof.

They reached the station. Nobody was waiting for Louise; nobody knew she was coming. At last, when they were driving in the cab down the Rue St. Honoré, M. de Bresse turned suddenly to his niece:

'I am afraid you will find your mother very ill.'

'Very ill! Oh! uncle, how can you say so?

Surely you have had no further news since we left Bressuire?'

'No, but this morning's letter was sufficiently alarming.'

Louise burst into tears. 'Oh! mamma, mamma! why did they not send for me sooner? She would have sent for me herself if she was so very ill. Why, she wrote to me only three days ago!'

'Eight days ago,' said M. de Bresse, thus betraying how carefully, if silently, he had watched for tidings of his sister-in-law.

'Was it eight days? Yes, I remember now. My last letter was from Anna, telling me about her walk to the Tuileries, but telling me nothing of mamma.'

'No; you have all been served alike,' muttered M. de Bresse between his teeth; 'and now——'

But that minute they stopped before No. 28 in the Rue St. Honoré, and Louise, opening the cab-door before anyone could assist her, leaped out, and darted light as a bird up the staircase. She was going to ring the bell at the first floor, when the door slowly opened.

'Thank God!' cried the old nurse, who had nursed all the children. 'You are here at last, Mademoiselle Louise.'

'Yes, I am here,' said Louise, taking no notice of the old woman's frightened aspect. 'Where is mamma? In her room, I suppose?' And she was darting into the *salon*, which opened into her mother's chamber, when old Catherine caught her by the arm.

'I don't wish to hinder you, child; but do you know your mother is very, very ill?'

'Yes! yes!' and, tearing herself free, Louise burst into her mother's room.

The noise she made caused her father, who sat by the bedside, to turn round. He saw his daughter, rose, and came towards her. One glance sufficed to show Louise, through the half-closed curtains, her mother's face, wasted and wan. Then, for the first time in her life, the poor child saw the awful seal which God sets on those faces which He is about to take to Himself. Uttering a cry that made the dying woman turn round in her bed, Louise threw herself upon her mother, and burst into tears.

'Mamma! mamma!' cried she, regardless of her father's efforts to silence her, 'why did you not send for me? How could you let me amuse myself, when I ought to have been taking care of you? You were very cruel. I knew nothing; nobody told me. Oh! mamma, mamma!'

'Louis, she is killing me,' said the mother in a choking voice.

M. Rambert took his daughter up in his arms, and carried her to her own room, saying in a severe tone,—

'When you have a little controlled your egotistic, selfish grief, you may return to your mother.'

Alas! nobody had ever taught Louise self-control in anything. She made vain efforts to calm herself. Anna and Caroline, terrified, ran to her, and tried to console her.

'It was mamma herself who forbade your being sent for,' said Anna. 'I heard her say so to papa one day. And did you actually enter her room? She told Catherine we must not come there. And Arthur goes to college just as usual. Perhaps mamma will be better to-morrow.'

But Louise, who had seen her mother, could not be deceived. At each word of her little sister the bitter feeling of injustice recurred to her mind. Why had she not been allowed to nurse her mother—her mother, who was so fast slipping away from her?

Old Catherine entered the room. 'Courage, child,' said she, caressing Louise. 'You have but a few hours to be useful to her. You can weep afterwards. Ask God for strength to calm yourself, and go back to your mother's room.'

'I cannot! I cannot!' sobbed Louise. But she accepted a glass of water that the old nurse gave her, and allowed her to arrange her disordered hair.

'You *must* do it,' said Catherine. 'You *must* learn to make some effort. Your poor mamma has hitherto had all the pain; it is your turn now.'

Louise grew quieter. She was choking, but she wept no longer. Poor child! every night and morning she was accustomed to kneel down and 'say her prayers,' but she had never yet *prayed.* Now—for the first time—in her anguish her heart went up to God.

'I will go back to mamma,' she said to Anna. 'Do you stay here; she may not wish to see you yet.'

And the eldest sister returned to her dying mother's room.

CHAPTER II.

MOTHERLESS.

THE last solemn hour was over: M. Rambert was a widower, and his children were orphans.

Louise alone closed her mother's eyes; neither her sisters or brother ever saw again her who had loved them as we are never loved twice in this world. The poor children wept together in their eldest sister's room. M. Rambert had shut himself up in his study. Already it was felt by all that the centre—the heart—of the family was gone. Louise tried to pray—tried also to read some verses out of the Bible: a vague need seemed to thrust her towards Divine help; but, in spite of her serious thoughts, in spite of her grief, wonderings concerning the past and the future came unceasingly to her mind.

'Why,' thought she, 'did papa wish to nurse mamma all alone? Or was it mamma who was afraid of doing us harm? What is to become of us all? Who is to manage the house?'

And unconsciously a certain vague idea of importance awoke in the young girl's heart. She thought over all she had now to do, but she never asked herself how she was going to do it; nor did it occur to her to pray for strength to fulfil so many new duties, quite beyond her age.

For some days M. Rambert shut himself up in his solitude, only seeing his children at meal-times; and these even he avoided by often going out just before breakfast or dinner. M. de Bresse had come to Paris to pay the last respect to his sister-in-law, and his wife at Bressuire waited impatiently for M. Rambert to say a word that would permit her to come and assist him in the new and painful re-organisation of his household. But he said nothing, wrote nothing, and Madame de Bresse knew too well his suspicious temperament to offer counsels or services that were unasked.

At last, in about a week, domestic confusion followed sickness and death. Louise had given the necessary orders for mourning without daring to consult her father; and she knew not how to ask him for the money, that she might pay for her own dresses and her sisters', until one morning old Catherine entered resolutely into the study. M. Rambert was seated in front of his desk, a pile of unopened letters before him, his head resting on his hands. Catherine placed beside him a cup of chocolate.

'Monsieur,' said she, 'here is your breakfast, since you never breakfast with the children.'

Her master raised his head: 'What were you saying? I want nothing.'

'Yes, Monsieur, you do. You cannot go fasting all day long if you wish to remain with your children. Who knows what will become of them? Mademoiselle Louise already looks quite bewildered.'

'Louise? Ah! poor children; life is now hard for them, as it is for me. *She* used to spoil us all.'

M. Rambert let his head fall again upon his hands. Catherine would have said more, but she respected her master's sorrow. She herself would not weep; yet Madame Rambert had been the person whom Catherine loved best in all the world.

The old woman's words bore fruit. In the midst of his sad absorption M. Rambert remembered how his wife had dreaded the thought of darkening the bright youth of her children— how she tried to spare them all grief and trouble. This remembrance helped him to rouse himself. At breakfast-time he entered the dining-room. Arthur was not there; he always breakfasted with his tutor, and departed without seeing his father, who until now had never encouraged any marks of affection from the children. Anna and Caroline sat by Louise; the poor things seemed all huddling up to one another.

'Here is papa!' said Anna in a low voice, looking very much astonished.

The three girls rose timidly; their father came forward and kissed them. The meal began in silence; but when Louise brought him his cup of tea, M. Rambert lifted his eyes:

'After breakfast, Louise, you may come and speak to me in my study.'

The young girl had longed for this; she had been wondering what her papa meant to do. The idea of a governess presented itself to her mind, but was indignantly repelled.

'I am quite old enough to keep house,' said

she to herself. 'We can go to classes or have masters as before. Catherine is here to walk out with us, and nurse us if we are ill. Papa will see how well I can keep accounts. What should we do with a stranger in this house? She would worry everybody to death. And am I a child to obey the first comer?'

All these thoughts filled Louise's little head when she entered the study. Without intending or knowing it, her looks were animated, and expectation was written on her countenance. Her father, raising his eyes, was struck with this new expression on his daughter's face, and his mind was made up.

'She wants to undertake the management of everything,' thought he. 'Poor child! I may well give her this pleasure—she will not have many others; and I could not endure to see a strange woman in my house.' 'My dear,' added he aloud, making Louise sit down beside him, 'I at first thought of taking a governess for you and your sisters; but I believe you have no great wish that way.'

'Oh! no, papa. We want nobody. I can do quite well.'

'You don't know what you can do, nor I neither. Sometimes I thought of sending you all three to your aunt at Bressuire, and keeping Arthur with me. Old Catherine could wait upon us sufficiently.'

'Papa, please don't send us to Bressuire. I am fond of my aunt: she is very good, and she is like mamma — a little; but she has such a small house, and to live all the year round in the country is so tiresome! They never see anybody, because uncle cannot be disturbed. One is alone all day long.'

'I shall be alone all my life,' said M. Rambert to himself. But he added aloud, 'If you are afraid of getting dull at Bressuire, you had better remain at home. We will try to manage as well as we can. You will order dinner, and

Catherine will tell you the price of things; besides, your mother believed her cook very honest. I will get masters for you; I do not wish you to go to classes.'

'But they were so amusing, papa.'

'They were all very well when she—your mother—could take you there; now they are not to be thought of. I will desire Catherine to stay in the room with her sewing while you are taking your lessons.'

Catherine! thought Louise contemptuously. What should Catherine do at lesson time? I verily believe papa thinks I require a nurse still.

'Have you any money?' asked M. Rambert, after a moment of silence.

'No, papa. My next allowance is not due, and I have spent all I had in hand.'

'Then I will give you fifteen hundred francs yearly for your dress—yours and your sisters'. As for the housekeeping, bring me your accounts every Saturday, as your mother used to do.

Ours will be a dreary life, my child; but we must do what we can for one another.'

'Oh papa!' cried Louise, with her eyes full of tears.

The weight which had fallen upon her young shoulders began to frighten her a little, but she was just sixteen—an age when we doubt nothing—and the love of power was strong enough in her to make her undertake her duties without anxiety. Nevertheless, many times during this, her first day of domestic sway, her mother's gentle image returned to her fancy—her mother who had never contradicted her, never imposed upon her one painful task; who had thought only of amusing her, of caressing her, of lavishing upon her every possible pleasure. Louise still imagined sometimes that if she were to enter the familiar room she might find her mother lying there on the sofa, pale and thin, but always smiling, animated, and ready to interest herself in what interested her children.

But Louise had never entered that room since the day when she had last kissed the cold dead hands and fled away. M. Rambert had locked the door which led to the sitting-room, and entered the death-chamber through his study; old Catherine used to put it in order afterwards, but the children were never admitted there.

Louise thought she could easily govern in her mother's stead and authority; but her sisters missed, more than she did, the constant tenderness in small things to which they had been accustomed. Anna had wept until her eyes were sore: her mother would have perceived this at once, but her father never looked at her, and Louise was far too busy to notice anything. Catherine alone saw, and bathed the poor child's eyes with rose-water.

'Ah! mamma is not here to do that!' said the little girl, pressing against her nurse's breast.

The old woman sighed, saying softly, as much

for her own consolation as the child's, 'No, she is better where she is. But, oh! what a blank she leaves behind!'

CHAPTER III.

THE ELDEST SISTER.

'WHERE is Louise?' enquired M. Rambert, entering the school-room.

'She is not yet awake, papa,' said Anna, rising to kiss her father. 'Shall I call her?'

'No. I can speak to her later on in the day. But why is she not up yet?'

'Perhaps she was tired,' said little Caroline. 'Catherine told me she must have been reading very late, for her candle was all burnt out.'

M. Rambert shrugged his shoulders and went back into his study.

Louise was hot and red when she came in to breakfast. She feared her father's reproof; above all, she dreaded his asking what book she had been reading so eagerly, and had a vague idea that he would dislike her taking books from his library without permission.

But M. Rambert was opening his letters, and had forgotten his questions and his displeasure of the morning. He sat reading his newspaper, and, absorbed in a great battle which had just taken place in America, he thought no more about his children. As usual, little was spoken at table. Anna and Caroline chatted together in an undertone, calculating Arthur's chances of being at the top of his class to-day. Louise was thinking of a new embroidered robe which she meant to work for the new baby at Bressuire. But nobody talked of either the plans of to-day or the reflections of last night.

'You may come and fetch your week's money,

Louise,' said M. Rambert, as he rose and went back into his study.

Louise, standing in the middle of the room, hesitated.

'I hate going in to papa on Saturdays,' she muttered. 'He has always something to grumble at about my accounts. Sometimes they are too much—sometimes the adding-up is incorrect. The other day he told me I ought not to give him salmon when it cost as much as six francs a pound. How am I to know the price of salmon?'

'But,' said Caroline, 'since you have to keep house, would it not be better that you should learn the prices of things?'

Louise turned round sharply. 'Let me alone, you little goose! I should like to see *you* with all the housekeeping to do.'

In order to escape from her sisters, she then went in to her father, who just raised his eyes from the book he was reading.

'Here is your money, Louise. And you can pack up your own trunk and your sisters'. You will start for Bressuire on Monday next.'

'Why, papa?' asked Louise, astonished, and not a little discontented by this sudden deposition from authority at the very beginning of her reign.

'Because your aunt has invited us to little Paul's christening; I cannot go myself, but am very glad that you should.'

'Will it be for long, papa?'

'I cannot tell. Probably as long as your aunt likes to keep you. Now leave me—I am busy.'

Louise went back into the breakfast-room. She dared not slam the study-door after her, or she would have much liked to do it. Why had not her aunt consulted her about this visit? Why had she been treated like a child? To-day was Saturday, and they had to leave on Monday. There was scarcely time to pack up their clothes. Louise vexed herself about these small things without confessing that the annoyance of losing for a while the excessive liberty she had had was the real cause of her ill-humour.

'We are going to Bressuire on Monday,' cried she, on entering the school-room, 'so we may as well shut up our books; we have only just time to make our preparations.'

'To Bressuire? Nonsense, Louise! Papa said nothing about it at breakfast.'

'No; but he told me when he gave me my week's money. And we may stay any length of time, he says, if my aunt chooses.'

'I hope she will choose, then,' cried Anna. 'I was beginning to feel suffocated in Paris; and, besides, there is nobody here.'

'But we shall look so ridiculous when our friends come to wish us good-bye and ask us when we are going to the country—sent off in this sudden manner,' suggested Caroline.

'For me,' said Louise, with dignity, 'I am

not so soon weary of home and of my duties. And I should like to know what is to be seen or done at Bressuire.'

'We shall see our aunt and cousins, and, since we cannot visit this year, we may as well be in the country as in Paris.'

'But how will papa order his dinner and pay his bills when you are not at home, Louise?' said Anna.

'Papa must do as he can,' Louise answered crossly. 'I did not ask him to send me away. Mamma never used to be so anxious to get rid of us.'

Thus harshly did the girl judge her father, ignorant that all that long day, whatever he was doing, he carried about with him the painful feeling of loss, and of the heavy sacrifice he had this morning made, in deciding to send away out of his house the only bit of sunshine that was left in it—his three girls. But M. Rambert was a silent, reserved man, and she who could have made him understood by his children was no more.

On Monday morning the trunks were all packed up. Arthur, who had been second in his class all the week, to his sisters' great satisfaction, condescended to approve of the journey to Bressuire, and even declared that he would go and see the girls there as soon as his work for the prize was done. He took no notice of Louise's discontented air, not having as much awe of her as her two sisters had. And Arthur, of all Madame Rambert's children, was the one who most felt his mother's death. His college life was just the same as ever, but his home life was altogether different. All his fondness for his pet Anna could not make up to the poor boy for the kiss at the day's end, the tender questions about lessons and school, and the thorough interest in all his doings which he used to find beside the sofa of his sick mother.

M. Rambert took his girls to Bressuire, but

had to return to Paris the same night. Arthur was starting for college at the same minute that his sisters were driving to the railway-station.

'Good-bye, young ladies,' said he, laughing. 'My compliments to all at Bressuire. If you find that I have profited by the absence of all my relations to run away from school, don't be astonished.'

A trusting look from Anna answered him. Her father had not heard the jest. Arthur ran after the cab till their routes separated; then he shouldered his packet of books and marched off to school. He was to dine that day with one of the teachers, and be back at eight o'clock, a few minutes before his father.

The warm welcome that awaited them all at Bressuire completed the effect of the cheerful journey through the wide sunshiny country. Louise forgot her griefs and wrongs. She remembered only her aunt's tenderness, the great trust that her mother had in her, and the pleasure they had all so often found in this simple home. It was with all her heart that she kissed Madame de Bresse, who pressed her closely in her arms, while Marie and Jeanne jumped about Anna and Caroline, crying out,—

'Oh! you've come—you've come at last! We have been expecting you so long!'

Then, in the midst of their delight, the black dresses of the whole two families recalled the loss they had sustained. The smiles vanished from their lips, Marie came close to her mother, and Jeanne embraced Caroline without a word.

M. Rambert had scarcely arrived before he had again to depart. Not unintentionally perhaps. He had not seen Madame de Bresse since his wife's death, and the strong resemblance between the two sisters affected him painfully. According to his habit, he fled away, to indulge his sorrow alone.

'Poor Louis!' sighed Madame de Bresse as she came in after having bade adieu to her brother-in-law. 'If he would only let himself be comforted a little!'

'Or seek consolation where alone it is to be found,' added her husband, laying his hand on her shoulder.

CHAPTER IV.

IN THE COUNTRY.

MADAME DE BRESSE had no governess for her daughters. Though Marie was fifteen, and Jeanne ten, they had never had any instructress except their mother. Even at Paris, before M. de Bresse decided on passing his winters in the country, on account of his love of books and of quiet, she had begun the teaching of her girls. Her two boys were at college*—resident

---

* 'College' is in France equivalent to school, and does not mean, as generally with us, some university.

boarders, to her great regret; but the continued stay of the family in the country rendered this indispensable. As soon as her nieces were settled down at Bressuire Madame de Bresse spoke of lessons.

'I should like to make two classes of you— Louise, Anna, and Marie in the first, Caroline and Jeanne in the second. We shall see which of the little madcaps will work the hardest.'

Anna regarded Louise with some disquietude. She was of an observant nature, and fancied Louise looked shocked to see herself placed on the same level as her younger sister. In truth, a slight cloud did pass over the elder girl's face, but she knew her aunt was not accustomed to have her intentions discussed. She therefore said nothing, but amused herself in thinking how her own superior acquirements would astonish her mistress and fellow-pupils.

The first few days all went well. Louise worked energetically; Anna and Caroline busied themselves in comparing their tasks with those of their cousins; Madame de Bresse declared herself delighted with her school. After lessons were over little Paul was brought in to amuse the scholars: each of them took him in her arms, discussed the colour of his eyes, or tried to discover whether he was not learning to smile already. In truth, baby might have suffered severely from the attentions of all his young nurses if, after a quarter of an hour, mamma had not carried him remorselessly away.

The christening day approached. Louise worked with all her might in the little room where the girls spent their early morning. Her robe advanced rapidly; so did a mantle which Marie and Jeanne were embroidering; so did a cap, made by Anna and Caroline between them (happily for poor Caroline she had only the half of it to do, embroidery being still for her a very serious business).

'Oh! Louise,' cried she one morning, three days

before the christening, 'what is to become of me? I have torn my muslin!'

'The more stupid you!' answered Louise, taking the little cap roughly in her hands. 'I have done the half of your work for you, and now, just at the end, when there is scarcely time to finish it, you have given me more than a day's labour.'

Marie rose up. 'Let me look at it. Is it very bad?'

'She has lost the piece she tore. I must make a patch and join the muslin, and embroider it over again. Another time, Caroline, you shall not do a stitch yourself. You are too provoking.'

Caroline began to cry. 'But I like to do something. I am six years younger than you, Louise, and of course I cannot sew so well. Mamma used to arrange my work for me without scolding me, because she knew I did my best and took pains with it.'

The thought of her mother smote Louise to the quick. She remembered how patiently her own little hands had been guided, when she was younger and more awkward at her needle than Caroline. She bent her head in silence, and, taking again the cap, which she had thrown down to the very bottom of her work-basket, she began to mend it quietly. Meantime, Marie, making a sign to Jeanne, had taken the robe which Louise was embroidering and worked diligently at it. Louise herself, absorbed in her mending, did not notice this; but Caroline, who was quite consoled by seeing the result of her tears, and had now nothing at all to do, cried out suddenly,—

'See! Marie is working at Louise's robe!'

'Why give yourself that trouble?' Louise said, just lifting her eyes. 'My good Marie, I can manage the matter by sitting up a little later than usual to-night. I am obliged to do this mending by daylight, but I can embroider by candlelight.'

'No, no: mamma says this is bad for the eyes.'

'Oh, in Paris I always embroider of evenings. The allowance papa gives us is not enough to afford our buying embroidery-work, and I cannot possibly do without it.'

'I can,' Marie said. 'There are many things I want worse. I always wear my collars plain. But our mantle is nearly finished, and, as it has not taken so long to make as your robe, it will not require washing.'

So the two elder girls completed their work just as the clock struck the hour of lessons, and Madame de Bresse entered the room with baby in her arms. All the girls wished to take him, but Master Paul was in a bad humour and began to cry. However, they were all soon seated round the table, and Madame de Bresse announced that she was going to examine her school upon Greek history.

'Greek history?' said Louise, with a rather disdainful smile. 'I learnt it long ago: it is children's reading.'

'Since you are no longer a child, probably you have forgotten it,' replied her aunt, smiling. 'As for me, when I began to teach it to your cousins, I found my memory was very vague upon several points, and your uncle gave me some books to read, in order to refresh my mind on the subject.'

'Oh, I have not forgotten one bit, aunt.'

'We shall see.'

Poor Louise! the result of the examination was not pleasant. Except a few anecdotes and the names of remarkable persons, she had forgotten almost everything about Greek history. Anna and Caroline, who had studied it more recently, answered better. Marie de Bresse, in the goodness of her heart, felt almost ashamed of knowing the story of Phocion more correctly than Louise, and of being more informed than

Anna as to the campaigns of Alexander. She even tried to avoid answering, but her mother seemed always to choose subjects with which she was best acquainted,—a thing not rare to the industrious Marie.

Not to vex her nieces, especially Louise, whose self-esteem she was fully aware of, Madame de Bresse shortened the examination, announcing that the grand (domestic) professor of history would at the month's end undertake another, after which a prize would be awarded to the best scholar among the five girls.

'An examination with or without books, mamma?' enquired Marie.

'Without books, as usual. You will have your notes and your recollection of the lesson overnight. Only, as I wish all your tasks to be done together, we will now go back to our history of the Roman republic.'

'Capital! for I am just out of it,' cried Anna. 'Only our master does not do like you, aunt.

After we have once corrected our exercises, we may do what we choose with the book: he never asks a single back question, which makes things much easier, you know.'

'Much easier, though much less useful, I should think. But now, young ladies, run away out of doors: you have just a quarter of an hour before breakfast.* I must go and put my baby to sleep.'

With so much needle-work to do, a quarter of an hour was far too precious to be spent out of doors. In three bounds Louise had gained her room, and was finishing her mending, while Marie embroidered the last flower on the robe.

'How learned your mamma is!' said Louise, after a pause of silence. 'I don't think my mamma knew half so much. She never gave us any lessons: even when she was well, she had no time for it.'

* *Déjeuner*—at 11 A.M.

'Mamma told us one day that both her own and aunt's education was very much neglected when they were children. Grandmamma cared only for dancing and music. Your mamma danced beautifully, and you know how well my mamma sings. But when she married papa, and saw how he loved books, she tried to teach herself. While we were all little she had plenty of time for it, and now I think nobody knows so many things as mamma does.'

'My poor mamma!' said Louise thoughtfully. 'I remember when I was a very little child how she used to come into my room before she went out of an evening, and how beautiful she used to look, with her pretty dresses and her flowers. Ah! how nice it must be to be grown up, to do what one likes exactly, to amuse oneself all day long, and have nobody speaking to one about Greek history!'

Marie secretly wondered whether grown-up people were always "amused;" but she was not in the habit of discussing things with her cousin, and still less of giving her a lecture, so contented herself with quietly finishing Louise's work for her.

'There is the bell; let us go to prayers,' said she.

Louise hesitated. 'I have often intended to ask why you have prayers here every day?'

'Why we pray to God every day?' repeated Marie, amazed at the question.

'No, not exactly that. At home I always say my prayers in my own room, of course; but I cannot think why you all meet together for prayers, like a school. Neither papa nor mamma ever did this.'

'Uncle Rambert does as he chooses, of course,' replied Marie, slowly and gently. 'Still, I like our way the best.'

The two girls went together into M. de Bresse's study, where everybody was assembled. Caroline had profited by her loss of work so far as to go and run up and down between the espaliers in the orchard, and had there torn her frock against a stake, and crushed against her jacket a half-ripe apricot, which had made on it a bright yellow mark. Jeanne had lost the net for her hair. In fact, both little girls, in spite of Anna's care to efface the results of their madcap tricks, had been rather scolded by M. de Bresse. Both their poor little faces were very sad when the reading began, but as it went on, and as the good uncle and father knelt down and prayed for all, great and little, parents and children,—ill-humour passed away, and the two little naughty girls rose up with smiling faces, quite good and happy.

'I understand now why you like family prayer,' said Louise softly to Marie as they went into the *salle-à-manger*.

CHAPTER V.

THE CHRISTENING.

MADAME DE BRESSE had at first intended Louise to be godmother to little Paul. She wished by every possible tie to attach her niece to herself, to Bressuire, to the children; and all the more because the natural bond between the two sisters had been broken by death. But seeing Louise so frivolous, so self-absorbed, so pre-occupied by mere amusement at the very time when she had so lately lost her mother, she felt that it was impossible to ask the girl to take upon her, in the name of Paul, those solemn baptismal promises which she did not comprehend for herself. Therefore an old aunt of M. de Bresse, an excellent person, was chosen to stand godmother to his youngest son.

The old lady arrived, and was received with much respect by her nephew and his family; but the three little Parisians could scarcely restrain their bursts of laughter at seeing descend from the carriage, which had been sent to wait for her at Coulomniers, a tall, thin, dried-up looking woman, dressed in a gown of brown calico, much too narrow, worn at all the seams, with a shawl of green and yellow, and a Leghorn straw bonnet which had long lost all its shape. When the bonnet disappeared and was replaced by a cap, Louise could stand it no longer, but rushed from the room.

Marie, going upstairs to see if the trunk of Mademoiselle Ardouin had been carried to her chamber, felt herself seized by both hands and made to execute an extempore waltz on the top of the staircase.

'Let me go,' cried she, recognising Louise. 'I must go and see after the luggage of my aunt Lucretia.'

'Aunt who?'

'Aunt Lucretia. She got that name because she was born during the Revolution.'

Louise sat down on the staircase window-seat, 'Oh, I shall die of laughter! Such a dress! such a cap! and such a name! Marie, before you go, tell me where in the wide world your aunt comes from.'

'She comes from Orleans,' replied Marie impatiently. 'She is an excellent person, and I will not have her made fun of. Papa and mamma love her very much.'

'I don't make fun of her, but of her cap. Oh, that cap! Never can I see it without bursting into laughter. Marie, if you wish to avoid a catastrophe at dinner-time, ask aunt to send me my dinner into my own room. By to-morrow I may be able to bear it.'

'If you cannot dine with us, you may go without your dinner,' said Marie, and went downstairs to announce that the trunks of Mademoiselle Ardouin were in her room, already uncorded, with the maid waiting for the keys, in order to open them and arrange their contents in drawers and shelves.

'My keys?' cried Mademoiselle Ardouin, turning round. 'Oh, I never give my keys to any one. My dear child, I always manage my affairs myself.'

And, deserting her armchair, the old lady sprang up the staircase as actively as if she thought the locks of her trunks would be forced open in her absence.

'Mamma,' said Marie, when they descended together, leaving Mademoiselle Ardouin alone with her luggage, 'if you do not say something to Louise, she will make fun of Aunt

Lucretia's cap in her very presence, and Aunt Lucretia is sure to find it out.'

Madame de Bresse laughed merrily. 'Ah, that strange costume startles a Parisian. I am not surprised. For I myself don't see why, even if one wears a calico gown, one should not wear it as gracefully as one can.'

'But still tastes differ, mamma; and I am sure Aunt Lucretia believes herself perfectly well dressed. Papa will be vexed if she is made a joke of; and I own I would bear any punishment sooner than a severe look from papa.'

'You are right, child; I will see about it.'

Very soon, a few serious words from her aunt gave Louise the hint that her fun was ill-timed, and she must wait until she found herself alone with her sisters before she made a mock of the cap, dress, and personal appearance of Mademoiselle Ardouin, whom she persisted in calling Mademoiselle Out-of-the-World.

At six o'clock on Friday morning everybody

at Bressuire was up. Louise had to sew knots of white ribbon on the robe, which had been ironed only at midnight. Anna was trimming the cap, of which the last bit of work was but just done. Marie had finished her mantle, and now was helping her mother to dress. Little Paul's toilette also had to be made in good time, for they were to start for church at ten o'clock. He, however, was in a bad humour, did not concern himself in the least about the elegance of his christening clothes, and turned on his back when they showed him his beautiful robe or his dainty cap. Madame de Bresse was dressed before anyone else, and ready to dress Paul. Once in his mother's arms, the spirits of the hero of the day rose equivalent to the occasion, and he allowed his knots of ribbon to be fastened, his new mantle to be put on, and his cap to be tied—without any special outcry. After which, fatigued by so much exertion, he fell asleep on his mother's lap.

Madame de Bresse, afraid of waking baby, could not herself attend to the toilette of her daughters and nieces, but she trusted to Marie's customary exactitude to hasten the movements of the party, and it was not till a quarter to ten had struck, and nobody had appeared, that she began to fear the entrance of her husband, who allowed no dilatoriness. At last she heard doors opening, and Marie saying, louder than usual,—

'If you will spend your time in making yourself uglier than ordinary, I shall go, for I can't keep mamma waiting any longer to oblige you.'

'It is Louise who is so upsetting all your sweet temper, my poor Marie!' thought the mother, half smiling.

Just then Marie entered, very red; but she said nothing, and began to admire the sleeping Paul.

'Shall I bring your bonnet, mamma? I can

put it on for you without disturbing baby. How pretty Louise's robe looks upon him!'

'Why does not Louise come and see t? Are your cousins ready?'

'Oh, mamma, since they could not change their black dresses, poor girls! what do you think they have gone and done? They have been trying to make themselves fine by dressing their hair *à l'impératrice*, and, as they don't know how to do it, nor does Annette neither, it is all hanging down their backs still.'

'Take Paul gently and sit down, my child: he is too heavy for you to hold standing. I will go and hasten these young ladies.'

The entrance of Madame de Bresse into her nieces' room was like a thunderbolt. Louise had thought to make her first appearance before her aunt, in her hat, which hid the change in her hair; Anna's hair was still not arranged, and Caroline was putting on her petticoat.

'Make haste, children, or we shall' have to

leave you behind. I assure you, Louise, neither Aunt Lucretia nor little Paul will notice the trouble you have taken with your hair. Let us hope any strangers whom we may meet at Coulomniers will be more quick-sighted.'

Louise blushed; Annette finished dressing Anna's thick locks with very feeble imitation of the style *à l'impératrice*; frocks were fastened, hats put on in haste, and all descended to the *salon*, where M. de Bresse was beginning to be most impatient. Aunt Lucretia, in a costume more extraordinary and more sumptuous than that of the previous evening, was seated beside Marie, who still held on her lap little Paul. The look she cast upon baby was at once serious and tender: it was evident the good elder sister had been praying for the child, and all idea of careless jesting passed away even from the mocking spirit of Louise. It returned only in degree even when Mademoiselle Ardouin rose slowly, exhibiting to public view the enormous brown reticule that hung on her arm, and the handkerchief, embroidered with yellow silk, which she drew out of it to dry her eyes.

In returning from church after the christening, the two carriages were fuller than when they went. Amédée and Raoul de Bresse, having obtained special leave of absence, appeared at Coulomniers just as service was over. They had been installed on the box-seat outside, and their mother dared not even suggest to Mademoiselle Ardouin her fear lest the reins had passed into hands far less experienced than those of M. de Bresse and the coachman. However, the horses were old and quiet, and in case of any disaster the legitimate authorities would regain their rights; so she remained tranquil, in spite of Anna's occasional outcry when the wheels rolled against a stone. But the mother had ceased to be alarmed at her sons' tricks.

She could not help laughing, though, when she saw Amédée look gravely at Louise, and then vanish, solemnly bowing, from the carriage-door. She guessed some joke was in preparation. And, in truth, when the family had assembled to luncheon, after the fatigues of the morning, in walked Amédée, with his hair parted down the middle, and rolled back in raised waves which were not a bad imitation of Louise's new style of wearing hers.

Everybody burst out laughing. M. de Bresse alone did not comprehend the joke; but when he glanced at Louise he saw it all and laughed too.

'I did not know it was the fashion to look like the Chinese painted upon teacups,' said he.

And that was the end of Louise's attempt to instruct the Bressuire barbarians in the elegancies of the period.

CHAPTER VI.

PARIS ONCE MORE.

THE boys departed on the morrow after the christening-day. Mademoiselle Ardouin, after having stayed a week at Bressuire, went back to Orleans, where, she wrote word, she found her old friends, her faithful servant Claudine and her cat, in the very best of health. She did not say how she found others, who furnished the principal occupation of her life—the poor whom she fed, the sick whom she nursed, the sorrowful whom she comforted. Many a dark room in the back streets of Orleans had grown darker for Mademoiselle Ardouin's week of absence, and when she returned, laden with flowers, fresh vegetables, and a hundred other trifles, there was joy in many a garret of the old town.

Louise began to weary of Bressuire; Anna, too, thought it time to go back to Paris; and, besides, Arthur, who during his vacation had taken with his father a tour in Scotland, was back at home to recommence his classes. Caroline alone found Jeanne and the hazel-nuts more amusing than the streets of Paris and the Tuileries gardens; but she, being the youngest, was not consulted at all. Louise wrote to her father that it was growing very chilly here in the country.

'Anna has already sneezed several times, and I fear she has caught cold. Besides, dear papa, it is long since you were left alone without us; and Arthur ought to be anxious to see his sisters again.'

This mixture of good and bad reasons decided M. Rambert. Always sudden and silent in his movements, he never answered Louise's letter; but one morning he appeared at Bressuire, and desired his daughters to pack up their boxes, for he should take them home the same night.

'But why are you in such a hurry, my dear Louis?' said his sister-in-law. 'Can you not rest here a day, and allow the children to get used to the idea of parting?'

'At their age, sister, one is soon consoled,' returned he, with the impatient manner that he often had at Bressuire. 'You know I am always busy, and I want to have my daughters around me again.'

This reason was unanswerable; but Madame de Bresse was still not quite satisfied, and Marie, who had much acute observation, made a suggestion to her mother.

'Louise did not look astonished when her father arrived: perhaps she had written to him to fetch them. She must, then, have grown tired of us.'

'I do not think so, child,' returned Madame de Bresse. 'In Paris she can see no more society than she can here, on account of her mourning. It must be that she wants to go back to her father and brother.'

'That is quite natural, mamma,' said Marie, too just to blame her cousin for preferring Paris and her own kindred to Bressuire, with all its charms.

At six o'clock in the evening M. Rambert and his three daughters started by the railway. Caroline was crying; Madame de Bresse regarded her nieces, Louise especially, with a tender and sad expression, which they could not help noticing. Louise held her hand out to her aunt from the carriage-window, saying in a whisper,—

'I promise not to forget our conversation.'

Alas! before they arrived at the next station the promise had entirely slipped from her mind.

Meanwhile Bressuire seemed quite deserted that evening. When M. de Bresse came home he looked earnestly at his wife.

'I am not quite sure that we shall spend the whole winter here.'

'Why not?'

'Because it is far from impossible that duty may call us to Paris, my dear wife.'

At which she understood that he foresaw a necessity which had often occurred to herself, that she might be wanted with regard to her young motherless nieces.

Louise and Anna were delighted to be on their way to Paris; Caroline was consoled and wept no more. M. Rambert, during the short journey, read silently by the carriage-lamp. When they reached the Faubourg St. Honoré, Louise felt a pang at her heart. Six months ago she had returned thus from Bressuire to her dying mother. Now no sick bed awaited her; but there also awaited her no longer that gentle gaze which for the last time had been fixed upon her so tenderly when she entered that sad chamber.

Anna and Caroline had no such remembrances; they sprang up the staircase far more light-heartedly than Louise, while Arthur on his side leaped down four steps at a time to meet them. What embracing there was! what laughter! Old Catherine, beaming all over, was at the door, expecting a kiss from each of her children, and ready to go into ecstacies at their healthy appearance.

'Truly, I think you have grown,' said Arthur, walking round and round Louise as if she had been a monument.

'And why not, Mr. Arthur?' cried Catherine. 'She has not done growing yet; she is only sixteen.'

'And a half; don't forget the half; she won't. I believe she is not quite satisfied with my remarks. Tell me, Louise, have I offended your dignity?'

'Go away, you tormenting fellow, and let Louise alone,' cried Anna. 'Tell me about your own affairs. What new boys this half-year?'

'Oh, chiefly the old ones, except Herbette, who is ill; and his mother has carried him off to the south, I don't know where. But there's a new boy, come from Louis-le-Grand, who will give us a nice handful of work I think.'

'Why, what did he leave Louis-le-Grand for?'

'I don't know, unless that his parents were removing. He is a little fair lad, named Massy, looks just like a girl, turns white and red, and wears gloves. Yet for all that he works, works like a Trojan, without seeming to do anything. All his exercises are done better than any others. I shall have a pretty fight for it if I am to beat him.'

Anna had already vowed in her heart a bitter

hatred to little Massy, when her father looked in. He heard what Arthur was talking about much oftener than he listened to his girls.

'Massy is the name? Then I knew his father. A fine fellow and very well informed.' And M. Rambert plunged into his book again.

Arthur, after a moment of silence, continued his confidences with Anna.

'There is some stuff in the lad, I think, though he is too much of a dandy for me. The other day Paumeret was chaffing him because he came to classes with gloves on, and with one single blow of his fist, gloves and all, Massy sent him right into the middle of next week! Nobody thought he had been so plucky or so strong.'

'What a bad habit you boys have of fighting!' said Anna mournfully. 'Some day you will come back with one of your eyes knocked clean out of your head.

'Oh, as to eyes,' replied Arthur in a low tone, 'last week I had one of mine regularly bunged up, and, only think, papa was so busy that day he never saw it. Mamma would have seen it immediately. If I got a scratch no bigger than a pin's head in my fighting, even though I had never found it out myself, mamma would find it out. Poor mamma!' And Arthur sighed.

Anna sighed too. 'Ah! how good mamma was!' said she.

In truth, when the first delight of coming home, and the first talk with Arthur, were over, the girls all felt sad. They missed their mother much more than they had done at Bressuire, where they were absent from all associations that could recall her; her daily life among them, her constant careful tenderness. M. Rambert was sadder still than his children; but then he was always sad, and they knew not how to console him.

Louise tried to shake off this melancholy feeling; next morning she proposed to Anna that they should go and buy black silk dresses and velvet hats.

'Can we not wait till the middle of the day?' said Anna, who was busy arranging on her shelves some books she had brought from Bressuire.

'You forget,' said Louise, 'we cannot make our appearance in the middle of the day, with our frocks made shabby with sun and rain, and our hats all knocked about, after the style of Coulomniers. We shall be taken for provincials.'

Anna laughed. 'Well, and who knows us in Paris streets? Not a soul.'

'If you don't like to go out to-day, we will wait till to-morrow. As for me, I shall not put my nose out of doors after early morning until I am suitably dressed.'

'You may do as you like, Louise, and shut yourself up as much as you please. But I want fresh air, and I mean to go and walk in the Tuileries with Catherine for an hour.'

'As you choose. You will look just like Cathe-

F

rine's daughter,' said Louise, shrugging her shoulders.

Happily, at this moment M. Rambert entered the room, and the children never disputed before their father. Caroline alone began to jump about, crying out, 'I'm going to the Tuileries!' which made M. Rambert lift up his eyes. This frightened the little girl so much that she held her tongue during the whole of breakfast.

CHAPTER VII.

AT THE TUILERIES.

SCARCELY had Catherine breakfasted, than little Caroline began tormenting her to put on her bonnet and go for a walk with her. Now this bonnet of Catherine's was a great curiosity. When first she entered Madame Rambert's service—twenty years ago—submitting to the influence of fashion, she had bought a bonnet; and the children declared she had never had a new one since.

This statement had some appearance of truth, for the new bonnet which M. Rambert had given her with her mourning had already acquired the look of its predecessor, which was not unlike the headgear of an old quakeress. Catherine's bonnet was a source of great trial to Louise, though Arthur protested it made her look the most respectable of duennas. Still the sister determined there must be a grand reform before she allowed Catherine to walk with her in full daylight.

Meanwhile Caroline trotted along, leaning on her nurse's arm, and chattering to her about Jeanne and Bressuire. She loved Bressuire; but she also loved the pretty shops, and the regiments of soldiers, and the fine carriages that she saw in Paris streets. Everything amused her, and she herself was a great amusement to old Catherine.

'When I was a child,' said the little lady, 'I used to be so frightened of soldiers. I thought if I was naughty they would come and carry me off.'

'And you often used to be naughty, my darling. I remember one day, after we had been three months in the country, and you had had a great deal of liberty, the first notion you took into your little head was to go all alone down the Rue St. Honoré. I wouldn't let you—you being only three years old—and wasn't there a scene! You rolled upon the pavement —you screamed—there was such a fuss that I carried you under a porter's gate. The portress came out. 'This child is in convulsions,' said she. 'No,' said I, 'she is only naughty.' But nobody believed me. They brought you some water to drink, and I sprinkled you all over with it pretty well. Then your screams stopped —you were good in a minute; but oh! what a figure you looked as you went out into the street again! Everybody turned to stare at you —you foolish little girl!'

'Ah, you may well say that,' cried Caroline, laughing. 'Else I will begin again to scream and roll on the ground when I want to get my own way; but I'll take care that all the world is not looking at me. Ah, here we are at the Tuileries. What a number of people out! Everyone takes advantage of this fine day. How pretty the vine-leaves will be looking at Bressuire! There is a large vine growing against the orangery, and I always used to take its leaves for my nosegays. Let us sit down, nurse.'

Catherine established herself and her charge on two chairs at the foot of a tree, and took her work out of her pocket. The little girl went on chattering.

'If I saw any game of play going on that I liked, I would join it; but there is none. Stay, they are dancing all in a ring down there, and singing. I know the song, and they seem not to know half of it. I'll go and teach them.'

And Caroline advanced towards a group of little girls, who, all out of breath, were singing

'I do not play with persons who have not silk frocks on.'

and dancing, and proposed to them to teach them the right way of doing the song of 'The Laurel-trees.'

'There are a quantity of couplets,' said she, 'and all the laurel-trees end by pushing one another down.'

Two of the little girls had already taken her by the hand; but the child who led the dance refused to stir, and eyed Caroline over from head to foot. Then, with an air of disdain, she drew back.

'I do not play with persons who have not silk frocks on.'

The little girl next to her plucked her by the sleeve, and whispered, 'See, Valentine, she is in mourning. Perhaps when she is not in mourning she does wear silk frocks.'

'No, mademoiselle,' said Caroline quickly, 'I do not wear silk frocks, and I should be very sorry to play with such grand ladies as you.'

Upon which, making a profound curtsey, and

assuming an air of great dignity, she rejoined Catherine.

'Well, my child, you are soon back,' said the old nurse. 'What is the matter? Have the little girls gone away?'

'No; but they will not play with any little girls who have not silk frocks on. How that would please our Louise! She is quite of the opinion of that little empress there with her robe of blue silk and her hat and feathers. To-morrow I will put on my garden pinafore, such as I wore at Bressuire — though aunt thought it almost too shabby to wear — and I will *make* them play with me, in spite of it.'

'Ah! little girls are now as foolish as their mothers,' lamented Catherine. 'In my time they thought only of play. No wonder there are so many ruined families. When your mamma was first married she used always to pay her morning visits in a merino dress, and now ladies dress in silk and satin at every hour of the day. But look, child; what is that little boy doing? He seems all alone.'

'He is crying. Let us go to him, nurse.'

They approached the child; he had found a large horse-chestnut, which some one of the little greedy hands who always pick them up as fast as they fall in the Tuileries gardens had let drop, and was tossing it to and fro in a dreary manner, crying softly to himself.

'Why are you walking on so far away from your nurse, little one?' asked Catherine, taking his hand.

The child opened his astonished eyes. 'Nurse gone—me don't know where,' said he.

'What! gone? Where did she leave you?'

'To the swans. They eat my cake. Big soldier talking to nurse.'

'All alike!' muttered Catherine indignantly. And then she asked the child his name.

'Mi de Bi,' said he gravely.

'Mi de Bi? What is that?' cried Caroline. Perhaps it means Maurice or Camille.'

'No, no—Mi de Bi, Oriolé,' repeated the child.

'Possibly he lives in the Rue St. Honoré,' said Catherine, much perplexed. 'But what of that? I can't go knocking at every door down the street—such a long street too. Come, Caroline; people are looking at us; there will be a little crowd round in a minute. We will make the circuit of the Tuileries, and I will leave word at every gate that I have found the child and taken him back with me. Oh, I wish I could catch that nurse!'

Caroline took the hand of the little boy, who regarded her with perfect trust, and both of them went with Catherine down the walk which runs alongside of the Rue de Rivoli, when a woman suddenly darted in front of them.

'My child! my little Maurice! Who are you that have got hold of him?'

'Nurse! nurse!' cried Maurice, running to her.

'You're a nice one to have charge of that child!' said Catherine indignantly. 'Come, we'll go together to his mother. It is she whom I wish to have a little talk with—to tell her how you gossip with soldiers instead of looking after the child. He might have tumbled in the water to the swans, or been stolen, or lost! You wretch!'

'Oh, madame, Jean-Louis is my betrothed, and comes from our village,' cried the girl, who seemed only about eighteen, and was more troubled with Catherine's reproaches at her light behaviour than her want of care of the child. 'Jean-Louis was saying no harm. We were only talking of the furniture we shall want for our cottage when we are married.'

'Yes, and that while you might have lost the child. A pretty nurse you make! There ought to be a second to take care of both of you.

Give me his parents' address, or I'll get it from the police.'

Catherine had such a determined air that the poor young nursemaid dared not resist her.

'They are M. and Madame de Brice, and they live at No. 13 Rue de Faubourg St. Honoré,' said she, crying.

'Very well. I pass the door. We'll go there directly,' said Catherine.

Caroline, who held fast one hand of the little boy, while with the other he clutched his nurse's apron, cast imploring looks to Catherine, who would not see them, nor the trouble and fright of the poor nursemaid. However, on their way, she discovered that Mariette, like herself, came from Burgundy; and that—also like herself—she had been sent to Paris very young, to make way for six little brothers and sisters. Her heart softened. She began to listen to the supplications of Mariette, who implored her not to make her lose her place, and promised that, if so, she would never let Maurice go out of her sight, and would speak to Jean-Louis as seldom as possible.

'Only, madame, if he can save enough to buy a cupboard, I shall be obliged to thank him, you know; for that is a grand piece of furniture— and he will require to be the captain's servant before he can earn enough for us even to think of such a thing.'

'Let the cupboard take its chance—there is plenty of time for it; but take care of Maurice,' said Catherine. 'I shall have an eye upon you in the Tuileries, and whenever I meet you two steps away from Maurice I'll go and tell Madame de Brice directly.'

With this final menace Catherine parted from her countrywoman.

Mariette went home to make the best excuses she could, in case Maurice chattered of his adventure, and Catherine continued her way, enlarging upon the imprudence of mothers in entrusting their children to other children quite incapable of taking care of them in Paris streets.

'I dare say you were only eighteen when you went to your first place, nurse,' said Caroline mischievously.

'And perhaps then I was not a bit better than the rest of them.'

After which astounding confession Catherine went indoors.

CHAPTER VIII.

GOING SHOPPING.

NEXT morning Anna, having finished the arrangement of her books, consented to go out at ten o'clock to make the desired purchases. These were likely to occupy several days, on account of the necessity of being at home at eleven to breakfast, and the impossibility, according to Louise, of going out in the afternoon without being provided with new frocks and hats.

'Then why don't you go at eight in the morning?' suggested Caroline, coming in upon her elder sisters' consultation.

'At eight in the morning! What an idea! To meet all the cooks in Paris, who do their shopping as they go to market!'

'But the cooks won't eat you, and at least you will not be mistaken for parlour-maids, who cannot go out so early. Besides, you are too young and too foolish-looking; nobody would take you into their service.'

'You are intolerable with your quizzing and your absurd ideas, Caroline,' said Anna. 'I will tell papa of you. One can't say a word but you turn it into ridicule.'

The two sisters, to cut short Caroline's mischievous remarks, called their nurse, who came in anything but good-humour. She had been sweeping out Louise's room; she had to do the same for Anna and Caroline; and to put on a good gown and a bonnet was no joke to her. So she appeared in her mourning cap and her shawl, all ready—as she fancied. But Louise refused to pass the door-sill unless Catherine put on her bonnet, and, grumbling audibly, the old woman obeyed.

The embarrassment of the sisters was considerable. Their projects were so ambitious as to be stopped continually by the smallness of their purses. And when Catherine declared that what they wanted most was flannel petticoats, their own being so old and thin, they turned a deaf ear to the proposition at once.

'We will wear two or three calico petticoats, one over the other,' said Louise.

'And the washing will not matter, since papa pays for that,' added Anna, laughing.

So talking, they came to the door of the shop where they had decided to buy a silk dress which would do for winter. 'Next year we shall not be in mourning at all,' said they, almost without thinking of the loss of which their mourning was the now faint remembrance. For all the sadness of coming back to the motherless home had disappeared before the pleasure of their projects as to clothes.

Catherine alone was dissatisfied; she did not approve of these arrangements of her young mistresses—her 'children' as she called them still in her heart.

'Shabby merinoes, sold cheap because they will not last! Nasty onion-parings, which are called silk; very pretty I dare say, but let a shower fall on them, and you'll see! My poor children! who know nothing, and will listen to nobody.'

So grumbled Catherine; but her young ladies paid no attention. Delighted with their purchases, they returned home in all haste; but their watches happened to be slow, and M. Rambert had been waiting for his breakfast fully a quarter of an hour.

'Another time you will please to go out at a different and more suitable hour, children,' said he drily, when Louise, hot and breathless, took her place opposite to him, without even stopping to kiss him, as usual. 'I cannot be kept waiting in this way.'

'You will be reduced to go out of afternoons, or at the cooks' hour,' said Caroline maliciously to Anna, who, fortunately, was not so touchy as Louise.

After breakfast M. Rambert went out. Caroline looked for her books.

'You may go to lessons if you like,' said Louise. 'I have something else to do.'

'What is that? And what will M. Courton say to-morrow if our lessons are not prepared?'

'I shall tell him I had no time. I must cut out our merino dresses at once.'

'Cut out our dresses?' cried Caroline, amazed. 'Why you never made a frock in your life!'

'No, but I mean to learn.'

'I am very sorry for it.'

Louise grew angry. 'You had better not complain, you little thing—you who have the advantage of the economy without the trouble of making the dresses. For I shall not let you do a stitch, you are so awkward.'

'Bah!' said Caroline as she walked off. 'Since we have our allowance in common, all the advantage is on your side; it does not take near so much stuff to make my frocks as yours.'

Louise blushed; she too had thought of this lucky difference in height, but she was vexed to see that her youngest sister had considered it likewise. To get rid of the disagreeable feeling, she went to fetch a dress that fitted her well, in order to cut her pattern from it.

Alas! the table was big, the scissors sharp, the paper supple, but Louise had not calculated the difficulties of her enterprise. After an hour of useless efforts, she decided on calling in Catherine, whose counsels she had hitherto rejected with disdain—Anna and Caroline, offering a suggestion or two, having been dismissed with equal contempt.

'Are you there, my good Catherine?' she called gently into the room where the old woman usually sat sewing.

'Yes, mademoiselle,' replied Catherine, somewhat piqued at the way in which her talents as a sempstress had been despised.

'Somehow, I can't manage to cut out my pattern,' said Louise, ingenuously blushing. 'And my back does ache so with stooping,' added she, hoping to touch Catherine's tender heart.

'Well, then, take a rest, mademoiselle. There is no hurry for your dress.'

'Oh! yes, there is,' said Louise in a coaxing tone. 'If you would only cut out my paper pattern, I would cut out my dress by it, and begin to make it to-night.'

'And ruin your eyes with black sewing! But of course I know nothing about it. You can quite easily make your dress all by yourself.'

'No I can't. Do please help me,' cried Louise pathetically.

Catherine grumbled sometimes, but was never cross with her children for long. She rose and followed Louise into the school-room, where Anna and Caroline were at work as well as they could manage, being packed into a corner to make room for the big table, encumbered with the merino and the paper patterns.

'Oh, what a muddle of things!' cried Catherine. 'Go to your books, Mademoiselle Louise. I will carry all your rubbish away with me into the next room, and bring you back a pattern which has some common sense about it. Only let me be quiet, and go you to your lessons.'

'But I must have an elbow-sleeve; mind that, Catherine,' said Louise, seeing her merino all disappear in the nurse's apron.

Her exercise, however, suffered much this day from the exactions of her toilette: two or three times King Philippe le Bel was on the point of having merino trimmings at the bottom of his royal mantle; and the Knights Templars remained at the stake without anyone coming forward to set them on fire, whilst Louise was absorbed in meditation as to the shape of her bonnet, and the flowers which might be put on it consistent with being still in mourning.

At length Catherine reappeared, not merely with the patterns, but with the three dresses all cut out, and ready to be sewed. Once safe from her first difficulty, Louise—who was very adroit with her fingers—carried out her dressmaking enterprise with much credit. Anna sighed mournfully when this pitiless task-mistress made her unpick her seams sometimes, and exacted that the velvet trimming should be cut quite even; and Caroline revolted extremely at the body of her dress being tried on more than six times a day. But after ten days of assiduous labour, greatly to the detriment of lessons, the three sisters succeeded in appearing in their new attire, and Louise launched into endless calculations as to the money which was left to buy mantles with, and whether the milliner would give them credit for their bonnets until the next quarterly payment of their allowance should again fill their empty purses.

CHAPTER IX.

THE BOYS AT SCHOOL.

DURING Madame Rambert's lifetime Raoul and Amédée de Bresse, the two boarders at Louis-le-Grand, always used to spend Sunday with their aunt; but after her death they were often a long time without coming to see their uncle. M. de Bresse did not like to trouble his brother-in-law with having them every Sunday, and found another friend's home for them to go to. This arrangement did not please Arthur, who was fond of his cousins, and often did not know what to do with himself during his holidays. He was unwilling to spend the whole day away from his sisters, of whom he saw so little; indeed, Anna, who was sensitive in her affections, had always hot cheeks when her favourite brother accepted too many invitations among his schoolfellows. So poor Arthur generally stayed at home all Sunday, getting very tired of his sisters' company and his own, quarrelling with Louise, and reading all the books, good or bad, that he could find in his father's library.

He was therefore highly delighted when, one Saturday evening, coming in from college, he found that his father had received a letter from Raoul, explaining that the friend they usually went to was ill, and he would be so much obliged if his uncle would get them leave to visit him on the morrow—especially as it was 'honorary' leave, he added.

'What is "honorary" leave?' asked Caroline.

'Permission to go out on a Sunday which is not your turn,' said Arthur. 'Usually the poor little wretches only get leave once a fortnight, unless they are hard workers like Raoul and Amédée: then they have " honorary leave " once a week, which allows them to get a breath of fresh air. As for me, I should soon be dead if I were shut up as they are, in spite of honorary leaves.'

'Nonsense,' said his father. 'I am not dead, you see, and I went to the same school. Nor do I perceive that your cousins' health is materially injured. However, we will give them an extra chance of life; we will send Baptiste to fetch them at nine o'clock to-morrow morning.'

'Is Amédée a hard worker?' asked Caroline after her father had gone back into his study. 'Raoul might be; but I should have thought Amédée was too full of fun.'

'Well, he is not so bad as Raoul, who works every day and all day long, never lifting his head from his book. But when there is occasion for it, he studies like a mad fellow, gets quite off his feed, and does better than any one. But of course he suffers for it afterwards. Never mind! I'm glad they are coming: we shall not be so stupid as usual, and I shall not have to take a walk with Louise and give her my arm,—rather a dull way of passing Sunday.'

At half-past nine in ran the two cousins, with Arthur, who had gone with the servant to fetch them; but nobody was to be seen. The girls were not dressed: Louise and Anna had profited by the absence of lessons to dawdle over their toilet; and Caroline was busy attiring in her Sunday's best the doll Amélie, for whom she had an ardent affection which rather scandalised Louise.

Raoul stopped, looked round the dreary empty room, and sighed.

'Oh! yes,' said Arthur, laying his hand on his cousin's shoulder, 'things are not with us as they used to be. But what can one do? I try to get used to it.'

Raoul might have attempted comfort, but, like all M. de Bresse's children, he was naturally reserved and more given to act than to speak. He contented himself with pressing Arthur's hand, whilst Amédée was making all sorts of signs to indicate the duty of knocking at M. Rambert's study-door to say 'Good morning.' Raoul comprehended at last, and he and his brother went in to their uncle, who just lifted his head from his papers, asked what news they had from home, and then went back to his studies again, like a man who has done the utmost that can be expected of him.

Meantime the girls had appeared, and carried their cousins back with them to the school-room, where the three boys got into a corner and talked over school gossip. Louise read a book, or appeared to do so; Anna played the piano, and Caroline played with her doll.

'Do stop that horrid noise of your air with variations, Anna,' cried Arthur at last. 'Play for us instead that old psalm which my aunt used to sing at Bressuire, and which is so pretty.'

'Ah, Marcello's psalm, sung by Madame Viardot.'

'I never heard Madame Viardot, but I have heard aunt, and that's enough. Nobody could sing better.'

Anna declared she had forgotten it, but would find the music, and play the psalm all right in the evening.

Here Raoul asked what time they were going to church, and Louise answered, 'Immediately after breakfast,' which was just ready. In fact, Baptiste now appeared, with his napkin under his arm, announcing, '*Mademoiselle est servie*'— in due form.

Louise, beaming with satisfaction, took her elder cousin's arm to walk into the *salle-à-man-*

ger. For this mode of announcing a meal was a concession sometimes made by Baptiste, when his master was absent, to the importance of his young mistress. Otherwise, the old servant, who had been in the house when Louise was born, said obstinately, '*Monsieur est servi.*'

M. Rambert came in and looked perplexedly round the table.

'What shall we do to amuse these boys, Arthur? I have sent word that they will not be back till eleven at night.'

'Let us go to the Circus, papa. They are playing the Capture of Pekin, which is superb, and I shall be so delighted to see those horrid Chinese bombarded.'*

'If they keep to historical accuracy, the bombardment will not last long. But your notion is good. What say you to it, young folks all?'

* In Paris all theatres are open on a Sunday night.

Louise thought the plan delightful, but hoped there would not be too many people at the Circus, as Sunday was the day for the shopkeepers. Anna and Caroline declared that, shopkeepers or no, 'Pekin' would be most charming.

Amédée agreed in this, though more doubtfully; Raoul opened his mouth to speak, but said nothing. His uncle noticed his silence.

'Does Pekin not attract you, my boy?' said he kindly. 'Have you any better idea for our amusement?'

'No, uncle; only—only—if I may, I would rather stay at home.'

Arthur burst out laughing. 'Stay at home? Stop in the house all alone? Are you ill? are you afraid of catching cold?'

Everybody looked at Raoul; the poor boy felt nearly choking. At last he said, in a low but resolute voice, 'I believe mamma would not like me to go to the theatre on Sundays.'

Amédée looked uncomfortable. M. Rambert shrugged his shoulders.

'But, Raoul,' said Louise, 'the circus is not exactly a theatre, and we must amuse ourselves somehow.'

'Besides,' Anna continued, 'when we have been to church in the morning, why not go and laugh a little at the bombardment of Pekin at night?'

'You boys will not be so absurd as to refuse any amusement, when you are shut up in that horrid old box of Louis-le-Grand all the year round,' said Arthur.

'I don't think mamma would like it,' persisted Raoul.

Arthur regarded his cousin with some wonder, and not without a little silent admiration. 'At least, you will come,' said he, turning to Amédée.

'Yes,' replied Amédée, slowly and stammeringly, without looking at his brother. 'I don't believe mamma will mind it—not for us. If it were Marie now ——'

Had Raoul been alone with Amédée, he might have reasoned with him, and reminded him of a good many things, but they were seated at the table's distance from one another. He felt also that everybody was making fun of him: it was hard enough to keep to his own resolution without trying to alter his brother's. And, as it was past church-time, the discussion stopped.

After a quarter of an hour's delay, which made M. Rambert so impatient that he went himself to knock at the door of his girls' room, they appeared resplendent in new dresses of black silk, mantles, and hats. Louise took the arm of Amédée, Anna that of Arthur, and they started off. Little Caroline possessed herself of Raoul's hand, and M. Rambert, who never noticed his children in the street, marched ahead of all.

The service was good for Raoul, who felt unhappy, even though his conscience was at ease; and Amédée thought that church in the morning would somehow atone for the circus at night. Louise, who was quite of this opinion herself, kept him up to it.

At half-past seven in the evening everybody departed, leaving Raoul at the fireside alone, in company with a book. He thought the house was empty, when Arthur ran in.

'I would not go without bidding you good-night,' said he. 'I don't understand your notions, but since you have them, you are right to stick to them. Good-bye! I am sorry it is not a week day, and then you would have come with us, would you not?'

'That as it might be,' said Raoul smiling, and Arthur leaped down the staircase to overtake the rest.

The capture of Pekin was a great success in the eyes of the children, and Amédée declared he had never been better amused. He said it all the louder perhaps, because he could not keep his mind from wandering to his brother, sitting with his book at the fireside. In returning to college, so late that M. Rambert had to send with the boys a letter of apology, Amédée spoke much of the Chinese and their queer Summer Palace, and the perfection with which the circus actors had imitated their long eyes and their pinched-up little feet. Raoul answered gaily; only saying he thought Amédée would be very likely to over sleep himself tomorrow. When they had passed the college gateway, and bade adieu to Baptiste, who grumbled a little at having to take so long a walk late at night, they found the porter equally cross. But Raoul also found a letter from his mother, which comforted him for everything, and he was glad he had done what he knew would please her.

CHAPTER X.

THE GIRLS AND THEIR FRIENDS.

'I WONDER if Laura Marmet has returned from the country,' said Caroline one day, as she stood watching the rain—which fell heavily and incessantly—the grey sky, and the dirty street. 'It is more than six weeks since she wrote to us; surely she cannot have been all that time in her beloved Brittany.'

'She would willingly pass her life there, I think,' said Anna, who sat drawing under the window, making the best of the miserable light of a November day. 'Laura is passionately fond of her father, of the country, and of geology. With these three necessities she could amuse herself anywhere, she says.'

'She amuses herself pretty well even at Paris. She helps her father to arrange his ugly stones, puts tickets on them, dusts the ancient shelves, and copies everything that M. Marmet writes—very fatiguing work that! And then she scarcely ever quits her blind grandmother. I should be tired to death, but Laura seems always merry. I think she would find amusement even in sweeping out a room.'

'Very properly,' answered Louise, not without a tone of contempt. 'Her father is poor; they have but one woman-servant. No doubt Laura is obliged to do all sorts of menial duties.'

'She has to put her hand to all sorts of things, and to take care of her grandmother too,' said Anna warmly, 'but that does not prevent her from drawing extremely well, and knowing a heap of languages.'

'Still,' said Louise, 'she sees no society, and therefore has plenty of time for study. If I were she I would draw a little less, and trim my bonnets a little oftener, even though I learnt to do it my own self.'

'You fancy everybody thinks as much about bonnets and gowns as you do,' said Caroline scornfully. 'But Laura's grandmother is blind, and her father would not see whether she had on her head a hat or a pumpkin, so why should she care? And she always look neat; her collars and sleeves are whiter than ours, and she irons them herself. I wish I might iron my own collars; it would be great fun.'

Louise shrugged her shoulders. 'I'll tell you one reason, child, why I dislike your friend Laura. You never go to see her, or even talk about her, but you get into your head all sorts of absurd notions. What use to us would it be that our papa is rich, if we had to iron our collars, and make our own beds, like any chamber-maid?'

Caroline executed a dance round her eldest sister. 'I did not say it would be necessary, but only that it would be great fun, though, perhaps, not every day. And since you don't like Laura, I don't like your friend Mademoiselle Lequeux. She seems to me a very inferior person.'

'What an idea! when Aline has an English governess, knows how to dance, goes into society, never walks, but drives, and is so rich that nothing is ever refused her! Yet you think her inferior to Laura, with her merino frock that I have been well acquainted with these three winters.'

'I do think so, Louise,' said the resolute Caroline. 'You may keep Aline; I'll keep Laura. But now, I must go and dress Amélie, who was ill in bed with a very bad tooth-ache this morning.'

And the little girl went off to her doll, while the elder sister recommenced her work. Just then there was a ring at the bell, and Baptiste announced 'Mademoiselle Lequeux.'

Louise received her friend enthusiastically, and said how kind it was of her to come out this wet morning.

'Oh, the weather does not harm me in the carriage,' returned Aline. 'And mamma is ailing; she has shut her door, so I am obliged to go out to amuse myself. What are you doing there?'

'I was altering a dress,' said Louise, blushing with vexation that her rash effort to hide her work under some cushions had not been crowned with success. 'Papa does not give us much money for our clothes, and if I am to be well dressed I have to work a little myself.'

'Dear me! I send all my dresses to Mademoiselle Félicie. Mamma gives me two thousand francs for my toilette, but it is never enough; she often has to give me ball-dresses; and then I run into debt sometimes.'

'And who will pay your debts?'

'I don't know. Perhaps my husband.'

The frivolity of Louise was great; but her instinctive delicacy was a little shocked by this remark of her dear Aline. She changed the conversation by inquiring why Miss Brown had not come with her?

'Oh, she did come, but I left her in the carriage. Very likely she has gone for a walk to the Arc de l'Etoile, and will be back for me soon. Meantime, I want to speak to you about something which does not require Miss Brown's presence. You are sixteen, are you not, Louise?'

'Seventeen, nearly.'

'So am I—seventeen on the 15th of next month; and papa has promised me a ball—a girl's ball—since I am not quite come out yet. You'll come—you and Anna?'

Louise hesitated, and looked at her black dress. 'In white, perhaps, I might come.'

'You don't mean to say so!' cried Anna, who

had overheard the proposition of Mademoiselle Lequeux. 'When mamma—poor mamma——'

Tears choked her voice. She turned to the window to hide her emotion from Aline, who regarded her with an astonished air.

'Mamma liked us to amuse ourselves,' said Louise in a low tone.

'That she did!' Aline added. 'Often when she was ill, she used to send you to our house; and you remember the grand exhibition of conjuring that papa and mamma took you to once, when your mother was so much worse that the doctor came to see her twice that day.'

'But you don't understand that our mother allowed us to go because she could not bear us to be uneasy about her,' said Anna, turning round so quickly, and with such flashing eyes, that Mademoiselle Lequeux, accustomed to see her very gentle, and very much led by Louise, drew back quite frightened.

'Don't be furious, Anna, when I only wished to

amuse you a little. Louise, what say you? Suppose Anna stays at home, and you come to my ball? You are my principal friend, and, besides, Anna is too young to go into society.'

'Luckily!' said Anna, and went out of the room.

Now Anna liked society well enough: at least the little of it that she had yet seen. Her education had not made her think of anything very seriously; but she had a warm heart, and she had passionately loved her mother. Running to her room she threw herself at the foot of her bed in a passion of tears.

'Mamma—mamma!' sobbed the poor child. Her mother could not hear her; but God is never deaf to the orphan's cry.

Mademoiselle Lequeux and her friend went on talking in the school-room.

'Your father will never forbid your coming, Louise? Shall I speak to him?'

'Oh, no; one can't ask papa things at all

times; one has to pause and choose a suitable moment.'

Louise stopped, alarmed, herself, at the doubtfulness of her enterprise.

'What dress shall you wear?' said Aline carelessly. 'I have already decided upon mine. Blue silk trimmed in puffings with blue tulle, and a garland of white roses—isn't it pretty? Unfortunately you can only wear white.'

'Yes, and I have no proper white dress, even. Worse—I have no money. Papa never will give us a sou beyond our allowance.'

'Run up a bill with your dressmaker. Nothing is easier.'

'Papa allows no bills,' said Louise, blushing to think she had already broken through this regulation—that the new bonnets, already half worn out, were still unpaid-for, and could not be paid for at present.

'If papa forbids this, and will not allow that, you must lead a pretty life!' said Aline sarcastically. 'Why! when I want anything, I torment papa and mamma until they give it, glad to get rid of me. Try the same plan, my dear.'

Louise sighed. 'Papa gets rid of me much more easily. When once he says, " Let me hear no more of that!" or only lifts up his eyes from his newspaper and looks at us, not one of us dare open our lips again.'

'Oh, but I would not be so soon frightened,' cried Mademoiselle Lequeux, laughing. 'I only wish your father would come in at this minute, and I would soon get out of him both your ball and your ball-dress.'

While she spoke, the door opened, and in walked M. Rambert with a preoccupied air. He bowed to his daughter's friend, and then asked if Louise knew what Arthur had done with a book which he had taken out of the study?

'No, papa,' said Louise, blushing with a painful consciousness, and hastily offering to go and look for it in Arthur's room.

'Go, for I am in haste,' answered her father, as he went up to the fire, and began warming himself. There he stood, absorbed in thought and quite oblivious of the young lady who sat by the window, until a sharp voice made him lift up his eyes.

'Sir,' said Mademoiselle Lequeux, 'may Louise come to my birthday ball, and will you give her a ball-dress, for she has got no money?'

M. Rambert stood a moment, silent with intense astonishment; then he eyed over from head to foot the audacious young person who addressed him, and answered in a dry tone:

'Louise is in mourning. She goes out nowhere at present.'

Then he relapsed into his meditations, without troubling himself in the smallest degree about his discomfited adversary, who went back hastily to the window, and began drumming upon it with her fingers.

Louise entered. 'Here is the book, papa. Baptiste had put it away on a top shelf in Arthur's room, so that I had some difficulty in finding it.'

'It is well it is found,' said her father, so severely that Louise was sure her foolish friend had asked and lost everything.

'This was not my doing, papa,' whispered she, with tearful eyes.

'I hope not,' he said in the same stern tone, and quitted the room.

Immediately Aline was seized with a sudden fit of impatience for Miss Brown, and declared, as the carriage had returned, she must leave at once. 'I can do nothing for you; your papa won't hear of the ball; so, Louise, come and see me soon and I will show you my dress.

She hastened away, her friend making no effort to detain her. Then Louise went back to the school-room, very much vexed with Aline, who had so clumsily managed such a difficult matter;

and reproaching herself for not having prevented this interference at once.

'Papa was sure to be cross,' said she, without asking herself whether he had not a good right to be so.

CHAPTER XI.

A LEARNED MAN'S DAUGHTER.

FOR three days little Caroline had been tormenting her nurse to take her to see Laura Marmet, declaring that if Louise's fine friends came to see her in their carriages, it was but fair that she, Caroline, should have a cab in which she might visit *her* friend, the only one she had.

'But Laura is not your friend; she is four years older than you,' said Louise, contemptuously. 'She might be Anna's friend, but Anna only cares for Arthur.'

Anna blushed. 'And you as well, Louise.'

'Oh, me, of course; but then I am your sister. And even with me you don't talk secrets for ever, and go about all day long hanging on my arm.'

'It is you I am with all day long, not Arthur.'

'Oh, I am not jealous. I merely meant to say you were nearer Laura's age than that little thing Caroline.'

'I am not a little thing,' cried Caroline, indignantly; 'some day I shall be taller than you, I know! And if older and more sensible people than myself like me, probably it is because they find me less silly than you. I don't care a pin for your little girls in silk frocks and hats with feathers. I mean to go and see Laura, and I shall ask papa's leave immediately.

'May Catherine fetch a cab, papa?' cried she, running into his study. 'I want to go and see Laura Marmet, and it is too far to walk.'

'Laura Marmet, the geologist's daughter?' said M. Rambert, closing his book to listen. 'Yes; Marmet is a capital fellow so long as he keeps to his stones, but he knows nothing at all of this world.'

Caroline did not trouble herself at all about M. Marmet's capacity or incapacity for practical affairs: it was enough for her that she was allowed to go. And, this being Friday and lessons done, five minutes afterwards she had got on her hat and was persuading Anna to go too. Anna was half-inclined, for she liked Laura, and did not know what to do with her morning; but she was indolent and undecided: Caroline's rapid movements quite took away her breath.

'Make haste, make haste; I'll get your hat, Anna. No; it hangs up too high; I'll climb on a chair.'

And the little scatterbrain had collected all Anna's walking apparel before the young lady had stirred from her arm-chair. Then she executed such a wild dance round her that the elder sister was forced to yield. The cab was in the courtyard already, and Catherine repeating at intervals, like a watchman of the night, 'Two o'clock. Five minutes past two. Ten minutes past two. The cab is taken by the hour, young ladies.'

At last they started, and it was a long drive. M. Marmet lived in the Rue Pavée, in an old house belonging to his mother. He also owned a small farm in Brittany, and this was his whole fortune. Laura declared that her father liked to live in the Rue Pavée because it was a suitable address for an amateur of old stones; he himself, innocent of the joke, said that he had been born in that house and could not live out of it. His wife's mother, who lived with him, had become blind in the house, and knew it so well, even to every position of the furniture, that her loss of sight was a far less affliction to her there than it would have been in a strange place. Besides, at Rue Pavée, Laura had not far to go to visit her poor people: they were close at hand.

These advantages however escaped the eyes of casual visitors. Anna and Caroline regarded with amazement the tall houses, apparently inhabited from basement to attic, often the seventh storey, by poor workmen and their families. As the young ladies noticed the ragged-looking women, the pale, thin, squalid children, they thought either the street must have altered much since last year, or they themselves saw things with sharper eyes. Catherine, still provincial, in spite of her thirty-five years' residence in Paris, muttered between her teeth:

'If Mademoiselle is in good health here, she must have the constitution of an elephant. There is hardly a breath of air to be got.'

But when Mademoiselle, with her fresh, rosy face, opened the door herself, Catherine was quite reassured.

Laura Marmet was not pretty, but she had such a frank, gay, affectionate look that everybody who saw her felt as if they would like to kiss her, which Caroline did on the spot, almost smothering her.

'Oh, Laura, how glad I am to see you! How nice you look! How do you contrive to look so nice in this horrid street?'

'I don't notice the street much,' said Laura, laughing. 'Besides, are people always expected to resemble the places they live in?'

'No, or I fancy only coal-dealers ought to live here.'

'I have not the honour of their acquaintance anyhow. But come and see grandmamma, who is not very like a coal-dealer.'

In truth, nothing could be more unlike the outside of Rue Pavée than the apartment of the aged Madame Lupin. Tall, slender, of noble and graceful carriage, her infirmity had given to her appearance as well as to her character a gentleness and benevolence that might both have been wanting when the black eyes were dazzlingly bright, and the firm will was not enfeebled by the weakened body. Hearing her grandchild's step, her countenance brightened.

'Is it my Laurette? Who was at the door?'

'Two of the Mademoiselles Rambert, grandmamma, who have come all this long way to see me.'

'They are welcome. I thank them. I should like to touch their hands.'

Anna and Caroline, much moved, came nearer the old lady, who pressed their hands; then, drawing them nearer, kissed them, sighing—

'Poor children! They also have lost their mother!'

'And they have no grandmother,' whispered Laura, tenderly, over the back of Madame Lupin's arm-chair.

Grandmamma patted her little girl's cheek.

'And how shall you amuse yourselves, children? Is there a fire in the *salon*?'

'I told Pierrette to light it,' Laura said. 'But first I must give them some lunch. It is papa's birthday to-morrow, so I have just made a lot of biscuits.'

'Can you make biscuits?' Caroline asked, regarding Laura with great admiration.

'Oh, certainly, and I'll teach you: it is quite easy. And you must taste my jam, and tell me if it is good.'

It was excellent, and so were the biscuits— better than any in the shops, Anna declared. After lunch, while Laura went to see if her grandmother wanted anything, Anna turned over the music on the piano. It all bore the name of Marie Lupin—Laura's mother.

'I suppose you have no time to practise here?' she said, when Laura re-entered.

'Not much, but I do a little. Papa loves

music dearly, and mamma played so well that I should not be like her daughter if I could not play. Grandmamma, too, who has not lost her delicate ear, gives me lessons from her arm-chair. You ought to play well, Anna; you were so fond of it. Try something, if you do not mind our old piano.'

'Presently,' said Anna, 'but show me your room first.'

'Willingly; but there is nothing to see there, I warn you. I am scarcely ever in it. As soon as I rise, I go and open grandmamma's shutters; then I make her chocolate; then come back and arrange my room. It is not at all pretty. But, as papa is gone out, luckily I can show you his collections—the prettiest thing to be seen in our house, I think.'

Laura's room was not much better than a small closet. A narrow iron bedstead, hung with blue calico, occupied one end of it; a table, a dressing-table, and two chairs completed its furniture. In front of the bed, above the table, was hung a portrait in crayons.

'Your mother, is it not?' said Anna, looking admiringly at the sweet and noble face.

'Yes; my mother. She was so lovely! and grandmama too; but the beauty never came down to me, you see. Isn't it funny that I should be just like a little dried plum?'

'You are charming, anyhow!' said Caroline impulsively. 'I never saw anybody more attractive.'

'Thank you kindly, my good little Caroline,' said Laura, laughing. 'And now let us go into papa's study.'

M. Marmet's room was as large as his daughter's was small. All along the walls were glazed cupboards, some filled with geological and mineralogical specimens, some with books.

'Just look at those beautiful fossil shells,' cried Laura, 'and this collection of bits of rocks, which we lately made in Brittany. There is nothing I like so much as hunting among the rocks with papa. He carries the big bag—I the little one and the hammers. Sometimes I succeed better than he, for my eyes are sharper. And, oh! I am so proud when I have found some curious thing which he had overlooked.'

'Ah, indeed,' said Anna, not much interested in bits of stones ranged carefully in old glazed cupboards; she thought them very like the stones she saw in the street. 'But what are you doing with that big shell which lies on the desk?'

'I am drawing it. Papa is writing a great book upon certain species of fossil shells, and whenever he meets with a new specimen, I draw it for the engraver. See what a quantity of drawings I have here already!'

'And do you draw nothing else?'

'Oh, yes. I copy the little cups which the fossil shells are taken out of, and I colour them like nature. But that is not nearly so amusing as the shells.'

Anna thought even these were not a very exciting entertainment! but she had the sense to say nothing, privately consoling herself with the reflection, how very much more agreeable her life was than that of poor Laura. But little Caroline, on the contrary, envied her friend this chair and desk beside her father.

'Papa doesn't want me in his study,' said she sighing; 'and I should be good for nothing to him there.'

There being no more to see in M. Marmet's room, Laura now proposed that they should return to her grandmother, who would probably let them amuse themselves by looking over her drawers. In fact, she had already asked and obtained permission to show her friends many curiosities of the olden time—short-waisted dresses, ancient fans, and hats of antique style, which had accumulated by slow degrees in the vast dressing-closet, where Madame Lupin had stowed away all her worldly goods when she came to reside with her married daughter. The old lady listened in great amusement to the ecstacies of the young girls on discovering tight-fitting gown skirts, leg-of-mutton sleeves, and various other eccentricities of past fashion, which they had hitherto only seen in pictures. Their bursts of laughter were incessant, and might have been indefinitely prolonged, as shelf after shelf was rummaged through, by the light of a candle which Laura had brought, when Catherine knocked at the door.

'Young ladies, it is five o'clock. We must go, or you will not have time to dress for dinner.'

'Oh how provoking! when we were enjoying ourselves so much, Catherine. If you only saw what funny costumes we have been looking at!'

'I saw the people wearing them, and they

looked no funnier than you do in your hoops,' replied Catherine, drily. 'Now put on your bonnets; it is dark already.'

'Laura, dear!' Madame Lupin here called out, and whispered a question to her granddaughter. It was whether her young friends had seen anything in the presses which they especially admired. On Laura's reply, the old lady rose, and choosing a fan of carved ivory and an ornamental necklace, offered them to Anna and Caroline, begging they would keep them in remembrance of a blind old woman.

The two girls, much affected, could scarcely keep from shedding tears. Anna kissed the hand which gave her the fan; but Caroline, always the most impulsive of the family, threw herself on Madame Lupin's neck.

'Oh, I wish I had you for my grandmamma,' cried she, kissing the old lady with all her heart.

'All very well, if you were my sister,' said

Laura gaily; 'but I won't give up my grandmamma to anybody!'

Then the friends separated, promising to meet again soon.

'You must try to get over your aversion to Rue Pavée, Caroline; for you perceive I cannot often come to you. Grandmamma never goes out at all. You must take the trouble of coming to see us.'

'You are worth taking the trouble of going to the end of the world to see—both of you!' cried Caroline energetically, as she jumped into the cab.

CHAPTER XII.

SUMMER-TIME.

THE winter passed monotonously. To Louise's keen regret, her father would not abate a jot of his prohibitions as to visiting: the girls were allowed to go nowhere until their year of mourning had expired. Louise declared sometimes that this was a ridiculous formality —that she should remember her mother just as much in a ball-room as in sitting stupidly by the fireside; but M. Rambert, who gave his daughters excessive liberty on many points, insisted on being obeyed in this one. He was so particular, indeed, that Louise and Anna scarcely ventured to buy grey dresses instead of black ones for spring wear.

Their father apparently trusted his girls extremely. He never inquired how they spent their time; paid their masters, without investigating the progress of the young pupils; not once asking Anna to open the piano, or Louise to hem a handkerchief for him. He never interchanged an idea with his children, and seemed to have lost at once all hope and all desire to be intimate with them, in the true fatherly way.

The correspondence with Bressuire naturally languished. Louise had found no sympathy in her dulness, and her regrets for the same, either from her aunt or Marie. The latter especially was a little stiff and austere in her goodness, as some young people are apt to be. She only understood the quiet home life, with no duties beyond itself, except the care of the poor. And she had a great aversion to dancing, and was always ready to condemn sharply those who practised it even in their own mother's drawing-room, and with their brothers for partners.

'It is evident you dislike all skipping and jumping,' Madame de Bresse would say laughingly to her eldest daughter; 'but pray don't terrify Jeanne with your strong opinions, for she likes to have a galop with Amédée, and I like to play it for them.'

The indolent Anna ceased writing to Bressuire altogether. She rose late, her lessons were never prepared, she was always in a hurry and never had time for anything. Caroline alone kept up a steady correspondence with her dear Jeanne, and sometimes let escape bits of news and accidental reflections which troubled her aunt a good deal. When she wrote, for instance, 'It is an age since I have seen Laura Marmet; she cannot leave her grandmother, and whenever I want to go to her, Louise always finds some hindrance,' Madame de Bresse regretted the loss of that wholesome influence which a young girl, nearly her own age, but so serious and simple-minded, might have exercised over Caroline.

Then, again, the child wrote: 'We have our new grey dresses. What a pity that we cannot wear rose-coloured kerchiefs with them! Louise tried one on the other day in her room, but took it quickly off for fear Catherine should see it. She has begun to embroider a white muslin dress for next winter, which will be charming. She can then go out to parties, and she longs so much to see the world.'

The good aunt dreaded much the result of these fancies of the frivolous eldest sister about the 'world' of which she knew nothing, upon the minds of the two younger, who, each in her own way, were only too susceptible of external influences.

Louise had a pretty figure, fine hair and eyes;

but Anna was remarkably handsome — tall, slender, fair, with a superb complexion, and large languishing blue eyes that won everybody's heart. Caroline's features were so irregular that one hardly knew what they might turn out; though the little girl's bright eyes, full of spirit and cleverness, her expressive face, and her lively repartees, made her as attractive as either of her elders. But, alas! she was also in danger of saying everything that came into her head, and often saying a great deal that she should not say.

Twice Madame de Bresse had come to Paris to see her nieces, and twice the chilly reception of her brother-in-law had frozen the warm impulse she felt to give some advice to her dead sister's children, or make some suggestion to their father regarding the future. She could only be patient and wait the event.

'If God wills we will go back to live in Paris,' said M. de Bresse to his wife. 'But He must show us the way first. We will not spoil things by hurrying too much.'

Madame de Bresse also shrank from quitting peaceful Bressuire. During the winter she had lost her little Paul, who had died of croup at ten months old. She had never lost a child before, and the blow fell hard. Marie, though grieving much for her little brother, who had been to her almost like her child, was still more sorrowful to see that, even by the end of spring, her mother had not recovered the baby's loss. M. de Bresse alone comprehended fully his wife's sufferings, and tried to comfort her all he could.

Louise and Anna had cried bitterly on hearing of the death of the little one whom they had carried in their arms; then they dried their tears and forgot him. Caroline remembered him longer, and spoke often of his happy christening-day. Perhaps Mademoiselle Ardouin was the one who, after his mother, thought most of her little godson. But she herself had had a sad life, and she felt the child was happy in being so early taken home.

Madame de Bresse had fully expected her nieces, and Arthur too, when his holidays began, to pay her a summer visit. But M. Rambert, partly at the instigation of Louise, declared that he had missed his girls so much last year he could not spare them this one, and should content himself with sending them to spend a month with Madame Lequeux, near Versailles.

'The invitation has been often repeated,' he wrote to his sister-in-law, 'and it is convenient, for I can go out to see them of evenings without interfering with my own affairs.'

In July 'nobody' is said to be in Paris—(except twelve or fifteen hundred thousand souls)—and Louise and Anna began to sigh after green fields and liberty; including plenty of society, walking-parties, picnics, and so on. As to Caroline, for the last month she had felt like a poor little bird in its cage by an open window, that beats its wings and knocks its head against the bars at sight of trees and fields. She longed for the country, would have gone alone to Bressuire, hated the environs of Paris, knew well enough why papa would not let them go and see aunt; it was because Louise had said Bressuire was too far off. Meantime, she obliged Catherine to take her every day on foot to the entrance of the Bois de Boulogne, which tired the poor good-natured old nurse so much that she used of evenings to fall asleep over her work, to her great humiliation.

One morning, the long-desired invitation from Madame Lequeux arrived. Caroline declared that Louise had fished for it in a letter she wrote two days before to her dear Aline; but, as Caroline had not read this letter, and Louise confessed nothing, the fact remained doubtful.

Then arose the grand question of the toilette. For more than a month their new dresses had been ready. In going out of mourning, the three sisters had hoped to be able to make some use of their coloured clothes of the year before; but they had all grown so much, and, besides, Louise said fashion had changed, so that they could not possibly wear this 'old rubbish.' Their father had given each of them a hundred francs for extra clothes, but that little sum had been expended in advance, and now to the velvet bonnets must be added—still upon credit—a summer hat, their July allowance only sufficing for summer dresses.

'One would think we were going to spend six months at Leuçelles, and Louise makes her arrangements as if she expected to meet the ambassadors and ambassadresses.'

'Without meeting ambassadors, Caroline, it is necessary to dress suitably to our position,' said Louise, without lifting her eyes from the trunk she was packing. She did not ask whether her 'position' demanded that she should run into debt, and leave herself without a sou to spend, either upon presents or charity.

One Saturday M. Rambert and his daughters and old Catherine departed for Versailles. Louise had recently made an attempt to persuade her father to make their nurse housekeeper, and give them a younger and more fashionable waiting-maid; but M. Rambert refused, saying Catherine was a safeguard against his girls being too foolish out of his sight, and that he did not want a housekeeper.

Louise and Anna were delighted to go from home. Anna regretted Arthur a little; but then he was so busy just now, in all the heat of competitive examinations, that as soon as he got home and had dined he found himself so weary that he usually went to bed. And Madame Lequeux had invited him to come out every Sunday, to-morrow being the first Sunday. M. Rambert was to do the same, returning with his son on Monday morning.

He was very sad. This was the first time he had paid any ordinary visit since his wife's death. He recalled the many happy days he had spent with her at or near Versailles, where she had relations, and he took no heed of Caroline's little hand, which she slipped softly into his. The child's quick eyes had discerned the father's sorrow, and, without comprehending half its depth or bitterness, she tried to console him—but in vain.

Arriving at the station, the travellers found Madame Lequeux's carriage waiting, and were driven to a large handsome house, situated in the midst of a fine garden, designed half after the Italian, half after the English fashion, the numerous terraces of which, bordered with flowers, sloped down to a grassy bank, which also descended to the river—the Oise. There was a splendid show of roses, heliotropes, geraniums; several peacocks were strutting about on the terraces, and beyond was a large pheasantry, filled with all sorts of pheasants and other birds.

'This is quite a fairy palace!' cried Caroline, jumping down from the carriage, and scarcely noticing Madame Lequeux and Aline, who had come to receive their guests.

'A fairy garden anyhow,' said Anna, 'and I suppose the interior of the house equals the exterior.'

'Oh, I don't care about the inside, only the outside,' Caroline exclaimed, as, crazy with the excitement of fresh air and liberty, she began running as fast as she could down the terrace-steps to the aviary; whilst Louise, though a little embarrassed at finding herself for the first time in her life in a strange house without her mother, made hesitating excuses to her hostess, explaining how Caroline was so fond of birds and flowers that when she got back to them again she quite lost her head.

'Oh, let her amuse herself, poor little thing!'

Then the lady, advancing politely to M. Rambert, requested the pleasure of his company, and that of his daughters.

said Madame Lequeux kindly; 'I hope you will all be perfectly at your ease here.'

At this moment both Louise and Anna were anything but at their ease. Seated in the drawing-room with Madame Lequeux and many other guests, whom she had left to receive the new-comers, they looked round them and could not find a word to say. Aline, after a civil word or two, went on talking with two other older girls. The conversation turned on persons and things with which the sisters were wholly unfamiliar; and Anna began to think that, except the pretty garden, they might as well be at Rue St. Honoré as at Leucelles.

The visitors at last rose to depart, reminding Madame Lequeux of her promise to visit them the ensuing week, to which she replied in a whisper. Then the lady, advancing politely to M. Rambert, requested the pleasure of his company, and that of his daughters.

'I shall not be here, but my girls may go

wherever Madame Lequeux likes to take them,' said he, rather abruptly.

'That lady is Madame de Saint-Éloi,' observed Madame Lequeux when she had accompanied her guest to the door. 'She has a chateau not far from here—is an excellent person, with an immense fortune.'

'Which is excellent, she or the fortune?' asked M. Rambert, with one of his satirical smiles.

'Both, I assure you,' replied gravely Madame Lequeux, who had no notion of a joke; 'and she is going to give an open-air breakfast, which will amuse your daughters very much.'

Louise beamed all over with delight. This was her ideal of country life, with visits, pleasure-parties, perhaps even a ball or two. What a contrast to Bressuire! This lovely park, compared with the half-wild garden, and the orchard where they used to go and count the peaches! Instead of Mademoiselle Ardouin and her Orleans bonnet, these elegant morning-visitors! in exchange for those nun-like household ways to which everybody was obliged to submit, open-air breakfasts and drives in carriages!

Here Louise stopped. She did not attempt to push the comparison between her aunt and Madame Lequeux, or even between Marie and Aline. In spite of their toilettes, the owners of Leucelles would have shown to too great disadvantage; and Louise liked best to look at the pleasantest side of pleasant things.

CHAPTER XIII.

THE PLEASURE-PARTY.

SUNDAY morning rose, pure and sunshiny. At Leucelles the family had the excellent habit of not meeting until the eleven o'clock breakfast; so M. Rambert and his daughters had plenty of time to walk round the garden, admire the flowers, count the pheasants, peacocks, and Californian partridges; nay, they even descended to the bank of the Oise, and watched the little boats which floated by —some fishing-boats, others belonging to various houses near, of which the occupants did not show themselves the best oarsmen in the world.

M. Rambert was at first quite startled to find himself away from his books and his papers, and in this pretty spot, removed from the tumult of Paris, an unwonted calmness crept into his heart. His daughters almost forgot their anticipated dissipations, in enjoying the sun, the green leaves, the song of the birds. The soft repose of nature irresistibly lifted them nearer to God: nor was the effect of this Sunday morning's walk completely destroyed even by Aline's jests at their early rising—she never thinking of quitting her bed till ten o'clock.

An excellent but rather lengthy breakfast succeeded. When it was over, Louise asked, in more serious mood than she would have been save for her walk with her father and sister by the river-side, 'At what o'clock do we go to church?'

'To church!' repeated Aline, slightly confused. 'Oh!—here—we seldom go to church at all. Versailles is so far off—and—people may read in their own rooms if they like.'

Louise was not much shocked or troubled; nevertheless she had been accustomed to observe certain forms, and going to church was one of them. Her mother's long sickness and death had necessitated the young girl's living in comparative seclusion and quietness, and the ways of this wealthy, worldly household were, to say the least, strange to her, in spite of her vivacious temperament. All Sunday long, carriage after carriage rolled to the door, bringing other Parisian friends to breathe for an hour or two the fresh air on the shore of the Oise, or country neighbours—mothers, daughters, young people on foot or horseback. Louise, bewildered by all this tumult, remained almost as silent as Anna, who stuck fast to her elder sister's side, looking not unlike a frightened deer. As to Caroline, she had declared her intention of living almost entirely in the garden, like a bird; and she carried it out.

'We have beautiful rooms to inhabit indoors,' said she, 'but I don't approve of the owners; therefore I prefer to live out of doors. The garden is quite to my mind.'

Happily for this young savage—Aline being grown up and an only child—there was not a single little girl among all the carriage-visitors.

Arthur had arrived by the early train; he first took a condescending walk with Anna, then, finding in the drawing-room some young fellows he knew, who had walked out to Leucelles—he laughed, chatted, and strolled about with them, troubling himself no more concerning his sisters.

'Now we shall not get Arthur even on Sundays,' said Anna despondently, and would have liked to go home with him on Monday morning.

M. Rambert was somewhat disquieted. From what he had seen of the household, he did not like leaving his daughters under the sole care of Madame Lequeux, who seemed as careless and irresponsible as Aline herself. After dinner, when most of the visitors were gone, he seated himself beside the mistress of the house. 'Is your circle as gay every day as it is to-day, Madame?'

'No, no! only on Sundays. All the week M. Lequeux is in Paris, and we see almost nobody: just a drive or a visit here and there, that is all.'

'So much the better, for I began to think I must take my girls home to-morrow. They are not used to so much gaiety. It will turn their heads.'

'It is well you have changed your mind,' said Madame Lequeux, 'for Aline would be as unwilling to spare them as they to go away. Do let the poor children amuse themselves! You would not make nuns of them? Louise will soon be old enough to be married, and there are several excellent matches hereabouts—very rich young gentlemen.'

'Keep them for Aline then,' said M. Rambert.

'Oh, she is our only child, and will be rich enough to marry anyone she pleases.'

'In the meantime,' said M. Rambert, drily, 'I will thank you, Madame, not to put such ideas into my daughters' heads: they are still far too young to think about marrying.'

Madame Lequeux burst out laughing.

'How little you know what girls do think about, Monsieur Rambert! Why, they talk about nothing else—except perhaps their dresses. For me, I have always allowed Aline to say anything that came into her mind to say.'

M. Rambert ceased the conversation. He was less and less satisfied with the manners and opinions of the lady to whom he had entrusted his girls, knowing no more of her than one usually does of a Paris acquaintance—which means nothing at all. But Louise opened her eyes wide, and turned very red, when her father spoke of shortening their visit; and Anna needed country air so much, and Caroline was so happy in the garden, that the father decided to leave things as they were, only resolving to come and see his daughters as often as possible.

The two girls felt a little more lonely when, next day, M. Rambert and Arthur had departed; but their hostess and Aline, both good-natured enough in their way, exerted themselves so much to entertain the young visitors, that, by evening, they felt more at ease. When M. Lequeux came back from town, his simple kindliness completely reassured them. Caroline herself manifested her approbation by proposing a game of draughts with him, in which she beat him pitilessly: not wonderful, considering the good old banker had never touched a draught-board since his childhood. And Caroline was in high glee when he promised to bring her next day a pocket of bonbons, as the price of his defeat and her victory.

When the important Friday arrived, Aline and her guests had already discussed for the twentieth time their toilette. The dresses of the three sisters—all of pink muslin—had been sprinkled and ironed afresh: Aline had made a grand exhibition of her own, which was an India muslin, magnificently embroidered. She was determined to put it on, though her mother foreboded some sad accident to it. They all had much laughing over the idea of breakfast in the open air, possible rain, probable spiders, and the certain dancing, which would counterbalance all these other inconveniences.

'But shall we dance on the grass?' asked Caroline.

'I don't know,' said Aline. 'Last year, at Madame de Belleval's, we went indoors to dance; but that alters the character of an open-air breakfast; it is far nicer to dance on the grass.'

'All right. I don't do my steps over well even

on a floor; but on the green grass—Ah! well, I'll manage!'

The sky was dazzling, the four young girls dressed themselves in great glee, and, for a wonder, they did not keep Madame Lequeux waiting more than a quarter of an hour. Aline, who was short, stout, and rather vulgar-looking in figure, had nevertheless a pretty face and head, so that she did no discredit to the general appearance of the group.

'Young ladies, you look charming; you will make no end of conquests,' cried Madame Lequeux.

Anna blushed with indignation. Louise blushed too; but already she was growing accustomed to her hostess's coarse way of speaking, and beginning to find these sort of jests not disagreeable.

Madame de Saint-Éloi's château was an older and less cheerful mansion than Leucelles, but the park was superb, the elegance of the interior very great; and the young girls were enchanted to see a band of musicians taking the road to the little wood.

'How well Madame de Saint-Éloi manages everything!' said they; and Madame Lequeux could scarcely hinder her visitors from committing a grand breach of etiquette, jumping about and clapping their hands.

Anna's excitement calmed down when she found herself in the midst of a crowd of strange faces; she held fast to Louise's arm, and both followed Mademoiselle Lequeux into the drawing-room. Aline exchanged greetings right and left, stopped to chat and shake hands, without paying the slightest heed to her shy friends behind. Caroline proposed in a whisper that she should be allowed to go ahead and open a road for them all, but Anna, afraid of her nonsense being heard, harshly bid the child hold her tongue.

They had only got half through the room,

when Madame de Saint-Éloi proposed adjourning to breakfast, which was to be in the wood. The crowd moved on to the door, and Louise and Anna found themselves separated from their friends. But once in the garden, the confusion lessened, and they soon rejoined Madame and Mademoiselle Lequeux, whom they found surrounded by five or six other persons.

'My friend, Mademoiselle Rambert,' was all that Aline said in introduction, and the little group went merrily on to the wood.

It was a sumptuous breakfast; although served upon planks roughly put together, there was no lack of fine linen and silver plate, and the ten or twelve tables scattered here and there in the little glades produced a charming effect under the dark tree-shadows. Louise began to enjoy herself much. A girl who sat near her had politely tried to talk to her, and they discovered various tastes in common—for dancing, drawing, and especially travelling. Louise, who had never been farther than Coulomniers, heard with wonder her companion's accounts of Italy, Switzerland, and England, and vainly tried to match them by repeating all she could remember of her uncle M. de Bresse's tales of India and China, which countries he had visited in his youth, for the study of Oriental languages.

Two young men, this young girl's brothers, had tried to make themselves agreeable to Anna, whose pretty face pleased them; but Anna was shy, and the conversation dragged on in monosyllables till Louise joined it. Then the face of things altered: questions, jokes, and harmless pleasantries were exchanged by all the young people. Anna chimed in with the rest; and even Caroline, who had eyed the strangers doubtfully for a long time, at last deigned to make a remark or two, and even to give parries and thrusts in the stead of Louise, who indignantly made signs for the little girl to be silent.

The dancing finished what the breakfast had begun. All grew thoroughly excited. The orchestra, hidden in the wood, seemed to scatter delicious music, as invisible as if from the clouds. The girls bounded over the grass, chattered and laughed, and seemed to have almost lost their heads. After a grand waltz, Louise sank exhausted at the foot of a tree; Anna gave up as hopeless the effort to keep her hair within the bounds of her net; and Caroline was seen whirling round and round all by herself, for she had never got a single partner.

'Now this is what I call *living*,' said Louise, when she got back to her room at Leucelles, so tired that she could scarcely undress. 'If papa thinks he can put me back into my cage again, he is mistaken—that's all!'

CHAPTER XIV.

A GRAND IDEA.

AFTER a month at Leucelles, prolonged a day or two in spite of M. Rambert, who did not know how to decline Madame Lequeux's cordial politeness, Louise came home. It was now impossible, she again repeated to herself, to put her again into her cage. The Lequeux family would soon be back in Paris, and they were to meet often, either at the small soirées dansantes that were to be given regularly to please Aline, or at the theatre, or walking and shopping of mornings. The three sisters had made acquaintances at Leucelles with several other girls as wild and frivolous as Aline Lequeux, solely occupied with amusement, and unable to endure a quiet or uniform life—life in earnest. To be sure they had never tried it. To them it only meant a dull school-room, under masters and governesses as indifferent to their pupils as their pupils were to them; and still duller associations with parents who worried themselves about their children's health, dress, or good behaviour, thinking little of their intellectual growth, and still less of their moral improvement.

Louise and Anna, whatever the faults of their up-bringing, had known the tenderest maternal love; all their pleasures, all their tasks, were once shared in by their lost mother, and they could understand something of what home life might be made. Also, though Bressuire had seemed to them very dull, they could not forget the picture it was of a mother wrapped up in her children, and able to make them happy even in the quietest of lives.

Louise and Anna, therefore, had not the excuse of their young companions for being always gadding about, yet it came to that very soon. Their father, entering the school-room by chance, generally found it empty. Morning lessons were hastily despatched; any bit of drawing or practising being taken with them to the house of Aline Lequeux or Mathilde Labrousse, where they said they were out of the way of Caroline! This little woman had declared plainly that being only eleven years old, she had too much to do, and too many things to learn, to be able to run about the world day after day as her sisters did.

'I suppose you have finished your education, young ladies,' said she, making them a mocking curtesy. 'That is your affair, but as to me, I don't want to be behind Jeanne in my lessons when I see her again.'

'Always Jeanne! you think of nobody else,' answered Louise crossly.

'She is worth more than Aline and Mathilde put together, and is my cousin besides,' retorted the little girl with spirit.

Anna actually found a friend, to the intense surprise, but nevertheless satisfaction, of Louise, who had long since fixed on Aline for hers. Mathilde de Labrousse played the piano and even composed a little, so she fancied herself quite an artiste, and believed she had discovered in Anna a sympathetic soul; while Anna, who was really the better musician of the two, conceived for Mathilde an unbounded admiration. The two young ladies talked of music with an imperturbable self-complacency; criticised Beethoven, rather put down Mozart, and exalted modern operas to the skies, especially those which they could murder as duets. Anyhow, music was an improvement after the endless discussions on the subject of dress between Aline and Louise.

The latter had no longer time for sewing; she could not carry her dresses about with her to make them at her friends' houses; and her dress-maker, milliner, and boot-maker began to have fearful bills standing against Mademoiselle Rambert. This idea often tormented her, until she set it aside by not thinking of it at all, but occupying herself with the amusements of the coming winter.

One of their friends, Adrienne Levasseur, often astonished them by her accounts of her father's liberality. He was known to be by no means rich, and yet his wife and daughter seldom wore the same bonnet for two months together; their dresses looked always fresh and new, and their velvet mantles were of the latest fashion. Also, Adrienne wore twice as many ornaments as young girls generally do. Louise wondered how this could be, until one day she learnt the explanation.

The girls were walking to Rue Neuve St.-

Augustin, where M. Levasseur lived, intending to ask Adrienne for a sleeve-pattern which she had promised them. They had never yet found her at home when they called, and so were a little astonished when the porter told them to ascend 'au cinquième.'*

Knocking at the door, they distinctly heard some one speaking within.

'How provoking! Honorine must have forgotten to say we were not at home.'

Then a heavy step approached, the door opened, and Louise drew back at seeing Madame Levasseur in slippers and dressing-gown, with a very untidy cap on, and decidedly in bad humour. However, it was impossible to retire, so they went in, and passing through the drawing-room, where there was no fire, waited for

---

* It is perhaps scarcely necessary to explain that most Parisian houses are divided into *étages*, or flats, each a separate dwelling, and called 'premier, seconde, troisième, quatrième, cinquième,' and so on.

Adrienne, who soon appeared, in a dress of blue silk, with a new sort of trimming. Louise admired it, and said laughing:

'What a deal of money your father must give you that you can buy such handsome clothes, and change them so often!'

'Papa!' cried Adrienne, bursting out laughing; 'papa would not know whether I was dressed in cotton or velvet.'

'Then how do you manage?'

'Why, papa gives mamma a certain yearly sum for housekeeping, and all that mamma can save out of it she spends on our clothes.

This explanation burst upon Louise like a flash of sudden light. The want of fire in the drawing-room, the stale fruit on the dining-room table, the one servant, explained clearly why the mistress and her daughter appeared out of doors in such magnificent toilettes.

Now Mademoiselle Rambert knew well that her father was a great deal richer than Adrienne's. Without going so far as Madame Levasseur did in these pitiful domestic economies, would it not be possible to manage better, by asking M. Rambert for a fixed sum for her housekeeping, and gradually putting aside from it a small sum now and then, to add to her own insufficient allowance? This brilliant idea lay hatching in her brain for two or three days, when she communicated it to Anna, who, without disapproving of it, thought it would be difficult to carry out.

'Papa won't like it, because he never did it with mamma. She always used to bring her bills to him as you do, and I know they had but one purse between them. Suppose papa should be vexed?'

Louise had a reply for every objection: it would be the most convenient arrangement possible, and she could manage so that her father did not suffer from the economies that she meant to introduce into the house. In fact it would be the greatest advantage for everybody, and it would put a stop to the robberies of the tradespeople.

Anna did not much believe in her sister's capacities as housekeeper; she thought it required a much closer investigation of internal government in order to bring about any great reduction in the domestic expenses. Nor did she rely upon Louise's perseverance in anything, but, as usual, she let her do as she liked. Her own opinion once expressed, she retreated into the shelter of her natural indolence—a convenient resource, which avoided all discussion between the two sisters.

They were sitting at table, when Louise suddenly exclaimed, 'Papa, I have been thinking—'

'Thinking!' said M. Rambert. 'That is a remarkable fact. Let me hear the result of it.'

Though slightly disconcerted by this ironical tone, Louise replied quickly, that she might not have time to lose her courage, 'If you will give me a certain sum to keep house with, I shall never need to torment you on Saturdays with my accounts. I shall know exactly what we ought to spend, and this plan will be better for everybody.'

'There was no need of it in your mother's time, my child, and I shall take care not to try it now. I greatly fear the money destined for beef would go in ribbons. Who could have put such an idea into your head?'

'Adrienne Levasseur, papa,' said Louise, in a low tone and very much ashamed.

'Ah! I comprehend. Say no more.'

Louise obeyed, and, in contrition, was seized with a noble access of domestic zeal; but she soon wearied of it, there was not very much to do, and Aline Lequeux recovered her empire over her. Likewise, the still unfinished embroidered muslin could be taken out on visits; so Louise, availing herself of this excuse, usually went out at 2 P.M. and did not return till six.

At last the father kept silence no longer. One day he grew angry, and said to his elder daughters that he did not intend their lives to be spent so entirely out of the house, in interminable gossipping with young fools like themselves. Louise drooped her head and began to cry. Anna, who had plenty of spirit when those she loved were concerned, defended warmly her friend Mathilde, saying she was no fool, but very clever and very charming.

'Possibly. Then let her come and see you here.'

This imprudent suggestion opened a door not readily shut. When the sisters were out all day long, sometimes their consciences smote them for deserting their father and Caroline; now, for the time, when they began to remain habitually at home, all remorse disappeared. They surrounded themselves with companions, and were never alone. Every time M. Rambert entered the school-room, he found three or four young ladies seated round the table, chattering, laughing, or pretending to embroider. Poor Caroline was driven to take refuge in her bedroom, where she worked as well as she could—thinking of Jeanne, whom she had not seen for a year and more, and of Laura, whom she had no chance of going to visit, because old Catherine was quite absorbed by the requirements of the other two. Her great consolation was when Arthur came in and threw himself in a chair in his little sister's room, crying out with evident relief:

'At least, here one is safe from all those young magpies!'

M. Rambert began to feel that it was in vain to try and stem the tide of frivolity. He dreaded severe piety, and did not love it; nevertheless, things were advancing from bad to worse, his daughters growing up mere dressed-up dolls, with not a thought beyond dress and amusement.

He concluded that a woman might possibly know how to manage them better than he could, and after long hesitation he wrote to Madame de Bresse the following letter:—

'You have often told me, dear sister, that if I were perplexed by the bringing-up of my children, you would come to my aid, and that Charles also would not refuse to leave his beloved Brittany to do me this kindness. I know not if you will consider the case worthy of such an effort, and I shall think it quite natural if you decline to do for my children what you would not do for your own. But I am weary of fighting against an evil which, it seems to me, is corrupting all the young girls I know, as well as Louise and Anna. They pass their days in silly gossip, and think of nothing but amusement. Already I have taken them to several soirées dansantes, which in my young days would have been called balls, and whence we did not return till three in the morning. I foresee an avalanche of invitations: if I decline, the girls will get dull, and cease to enjoy home. Caroline—too young for all this folly, and who seems to me to monopolise all the good sense of the family—grows very fast, is thin and pale: she says she is quite well, but I am uneasy about her, and so is Catherine.

'These are my perplexities, dear sister. Will you come and help me? Will you take charge of Louise, and see that she enters society this winter with some amount of moderation. Will you keep Anna, who is only fifteen, as much at home as possible, and watch over my little Caroline—the only one of my daughters who puts me in mind of her mother?

'You knew already I dislike Puritanism—it annoys me more than hair-brainedness—but I believe a woman's hand is necessary to keep these young heads steady on their shoulders. And so I leave the decision in your hands.

If you cannot help, I must try some other plan. Your affectionate brother,

'L. Rambert.'

When this letter was written and despatched, M. Rambert walked up and down his study with rapid steps. Never had he made for his children a sacrifice more disagreeable to himself. He felt that another and a different influence than his own would be exercised over his girls; and he knew by experience that Madame de Bresse, gentle upon many points, was firm as a rock where her conscience was concerned. Why had he so often tacitly discouraged his wife's intimacy with her sister, and yet was now obliged by circumstances to appeal to her for assistance in the bringing-up of his daughters? It was very strange; and M. Rambert, though he felt compelled to do it, did not like it at all.

CHAPTER XV.

AT BRESSUIRE.

'HERE is the long-expected letter, Charles,' said Madame de Bresse, entering her husband's study with looks as pleased as if she were announcing some excellent news, instead of tidings which required her to break through all her favourite habits, and upset her whole life, without hope of gratitude from those for whom she was doing it.'

'A letter from Louis?' guessed her husband at once.

'Yes. Our poor little nieces are going all

wrong, some morally, some physically, and he wants me to come and set them right. Only I am not to make them young Puritans!'

'No; make them Christians. May I see the letter, Cécile?'

'I have a great mind not to show it to you; it is such a mixture of frankness and repugnance, which would have vexed me had I not known poor Louis so well. How unhappy he must have been before he could write me this letter!'

'Give it me, my dear; I know his peculiarities as well as you.'

Nevertheless, several times M. de Bresse grew hot in reading the letter, folded it up carefully, and returned it to his wife, saying, with visible self-restraint:

'The necessity of the case is clear. May God give us both wisdom and patience to meet it.'

Madame de Bresse pressed her husband's hand and quitted him. Long as she had desired the time when she could be of use to her sister's motherless children, she foresaw that it would be a most difficult and complicated task. It would involve leaving Bressuire indefinitely, renouncing the quiet repose she had enjoyed so long, exposing Jeanne to harmful influences. The bright side of it was, her being near her two sons at Paris, and her entire reliance on Marie, her dear and good eldest daughter, for whom she feared nothing in any change of life. It might even benefit her, making her less severe in her goodness. And thinking over all things, in the silence of her room, the mother ended in the mother's best refuge—prayer.

When Madame de Bresse rejoined her husband, he looked as peaceful as herself, and as well prepared to meet the impatience and the touchiness which he knew he should find in their brother-in-law, as well as his own loss in renouncing his beloved country solitude.

'I think I had better write a word of assent to Louis, and go up to Paris next week, to see his children, and seek apartments for ourselves.'

'As you will,' replied M. de Bresse. 'And shall you promise not to make Puritans of your nieces?'

'Am I a Puritan?' his wife answered, smiling. 'Marie, I grant, has some turn that way. But it seems to me quite possible to win over Louis's children without offending their father.'

So M. Rambert was written to thus:—

'My dear Louis,—Charles and I are at your service entirely. I shall come to Paris next week, to find apartments near you. Perhaps you had better not tell the girls beforehand, lest they should expect a severe duenna where they will only find a loving aunt. Marie and Jeanne will delight in seeing their cousins.

'Believe in the sincere friendship of

'Your sister,

'Cécile de Bresse.'

'Marie, we are going to Paris for the winter,' said the mother to her daughter, who sat sewing beside her, while Jeanne was hunting in the garden for the latest chrysanthemums.

'To Paris, mamma!' Marie dropped her work and broke her thread in her intense astonishment.

'Yes, my little girl. Your cousins need a mother sorely.'

Marie was conscious of a bitter thought at the fear of *her* mother's time and tenderness being taken from herself; but she repressed it with shame, and replied slowly: 'This winter, mamma? It is winter already.'

'Then we have less time to lose. You must help me in my arrangements. I shall go to Paris on Monday or Tuesday to look for apartments.'

'But papa and his books?'

'We must take with us all we can. And papa does not mind being put out of his way a little for the sake of those poor girls.'

'Are they ill, mamma?'

'No; but Louise is eighteen; it is time she should "come out," as the phrase is; her father wishes her to go into the world, and has no one to trust her with but me.'

'And you will go into the world with her, mamma?' cried Marie, more and more astonished.

'Yes, dear, certainly,' replied Madame de Bresse, smiling.

Marie was confounded. Whenever she had found Louise frivolous and foolish, she had charitably attributed these faults to 'the world' in which her cousins had been brought up; and now her mother was deliberately plunging into it with Louise. It was incomprehensible. Still, trusting her mother wholly, but doubting herself, she prayed that she might be able to live as Christian a life at Paris as at Bressuire.

M. Rambert, busy in his study at the Rue St. Honoré, little knew all that his letter had caused at Bressuire. Jeanne alone had welcomed ecstatically the tidings that she was to winter in Paris, near cousin Caroline. She jumped with joy all up and down the corridors, exclaiming: 'We are going to Paris. I am going to Caroline; oh, what felicity!'

'Jeanne seems the best pleased of us here, and I expect Caroline will be the same at Rue St. Honoré,' said M. de Bresse. 'I do not fancy Louise will be over delighted.'

'Perhaps not at first, but I shall not draw the reins tightly; and, besides, I believe any girl, be she ever so giddy, must feel a mother's love. And Charles,' she added, lowering her voice, 'I love my sister's children almost as my own.'

'And shall you care if they do not return your love?'

'They will return it one day,' was the answer, so confident, that her husband did not contradict her.

At noon, on Monday, Madame de Bresse

knocked at her brother-in-law's door, to Baptiste's equal amazement and delight. She asked if M. Rambert was in his study. 'No, madame. They are late at breakfast to-day. Our young ladies only came in from a ball at one o'clock this morning.'

The old servant's tone enlightened Madame de Bresse a good deal as to his private sentiments; but he opened in silence the door of the *salle-à-manger*.

There was a general outcry of welcome, except from Louise, who said at once, 'Aunt, what chance brings you here to-day? Papa, were you expecting her? Had she written?'

'I told your father I was coming,' said Madame de Bresse briefly, seeing the embarrassment of her brother-in-law. 'But do you not want news of Marie and Jeanne?'

'Oh! we know they are well,' said Anna. 'We saw Raoul and Amedée last Sunday. Why did you not bring the girls with you?'

Caroline, contrary to her habit, was silent; but she slipped her hand within her aunt's, who by intuitive sympathy turned to her, though answering Anna.

'I did not bring your cousins, because I only came up to look for apartments. We mean to winter in Paris.'

The surprise of the two elder girls struck them dumb. But Caroline sprang into her aunt's arms; not, however, without a glance at her father to see how he liked this news. From a certain expression he had, she fancied he knew it already, and was no hindrance to the astonishing step which had been taken by Monsieur and Madame de Bresse.

'But what says my uncle?' asked Louise, recovering herself, and too honest to express pleasure which she did not feel.

'If your uncle had not been satisfied, of course we should not come,' replied Madame de Bresse, relieved also that she had not been pressed for explanations, which could not be agreeable without being a little insincere. So she asked her brother-in-law to spare her an hour of his time, to which he readily agreed, and went to fetch his hat. In his absence, Madame de Bresse had time to feel keenly the evident coldness of her nieces towards her. She pressed Caroline closer to her heart, as if thanking the child for at least one hearty welcome.

Leaving the girls to think what they liked, she departed with M. Rambert in search of lodgings.

'We can talk as we walk,' said she. 'Tell me, are you in the same mind as you were?'

'More so than ever,' was her brother-in-law's reply; for the sweet charm of her presence exercised over him an influence which was a little lost in her absence, on account of his great dread of 'Puritanism,' which he attributed to her. 'Last night, Louise wore a dress so fine, that I am sure the allowance I give her can never have paid for it. I dread she is going into debt, poor child.'

'Let us understand one another, Louis. You forbid my making your daughters into Puritans, have you any objection to their being Christians?'

M. Rambert was a little embarrassed. 'Christians? No, certainly not; but you have a peculiar interpretation of the word.'

'Perhaps so. Let me explain my intentions with regard to your girls—and my own. You ask me to take Louise into society, and so I will—not only because of your request, but because, with her tastes and temperament, I would have done the same had she been my own daughter. I think society dangerous—more so to women than to men, who are not tempted by feminine trivialities, such as dress and the like; but I believe also that resistance to this danger comes from within and not from without, and in that case only is worth anything. Marie fears and dislikes gaiety, so I will leave her quiet at home; but if Jeanne likes to go into the world, and find out for herself what are called its pleasures, I shall not refuse her. We must not lay upon our children burthens heavier than they can bear. We must not lead them to suppose the world is delightful, simply because its doors are shut upon them. Nevertheless, if I could choose, I would rather both your girls and mine were, voluntarily, *not* of the world.'

'So would I, perhaps,' said M. Rambert, recalling all the anxieties Louise had already caused him.

Two hours after, Madame de Bresse having found lodgings in the Rue d'Anjou, was on her way back to Bressuire; whilst M. Rambert, once more shut up in his study, kept turning over and over in his mind his conversation with her. Her strictness in some points annoyed him; but, at the bottom of his heart, he preferred even this to the career of future folly which, he foresaw, would be the lot of Louise and Anna, if they went on the ways they had so early begun.

'Anyhow,' he said to himself, 'there is a good step between what Louise is now and Puritanism. We shall at least have time to consider the matter.'

CHAPTER XVI.

COUNTRY COUSINS.

MADAME DE BRESSE arrived in Paris within a week—a week too busy for regrets. M. de Bresse was certainly the one who lost most and gained least—quitting his peaceful study with his innumerable books around him, for a furnished lodging where his wife could with difficulty stow away two hundred volumes, while his sole compensation for the difficulties sure to arise with his brother-in-law was the society of renowned Oriental scholars. For his wife—she left her pretty house, her poor pensioners, some very dear to her—the ease and comparative luxury in which she lived at Bressuire, for the Paris life, much more expensive, and infinitely less comfortable. Still, she had grieved so much these two years over the separation between herself and her nieces, that, now it was ended, the load seemed taken from her; she was ready to bear and to risk a great deal in order to gain the privilege she had so much desired, of taking the mother's place with these girls. Also, her last conversation with her brother-in-law had left behind the pleasant impression, that he not only needed her, but recognised the fact.

Her children were of diverse opinions. The boys were very glad, though Amédée complained a little at the long daily walk between Rue d'Anjou and Louis-le-grand; ending all his grumblings, however, with the exclamation, 'Never mind, we shall be at home and not in our cage.'

Raoul had feared this great change would not suit his mother; but, when he was satisfied on this head, his joy was very great, all the greater for being undemonstrative. Marie too was content. Perhaps, in the bottom of her heart, she would have been sorry had the Paris plan been quite given up. She was only seventeen after all—it was eight years since she had lived in Paris—and the new world that opened before her attracted, while it a little frightened, her. She was curious to see and know a heap of things, and she said to herself that, from all evil things, God would protect her—and so would her mother.

As for little Jeanne, she was quite crazy with joy.

On Tuesday, December 13, Bressuire was shut up, and the villagers slowly watched the departure of the carriage which took away their best friends, feeling that the winter would be hard to bear, in spite of all the precautions Madame de Bresse had taken that her poor should not suffer in her absence.

'What are they going to Paris for?' said one infirm old woman.

'To take care of Mademoiselles Rambert,' was the answer.

'Can't their father do that himself?'—An opinion in which Louise and Anna would have quite coincided.

After long conferences with their companions, these young ladies had come pretty near the truth, and felt convinced that their aunt had not come to Paris of her own accord, or for her own pleasure, but from some suggestion or request of their father's. They never took into consideration what his pain must have been, nor his anxiety over them; they only felt that their liberty was abridged, and determined to resist the aggression. Louise did, at least. Anna let things go, carelessly, as was her way.

'I suppose aunt has come to get masters for

Marie and Jeanne, and will be absorbed in lessons,' said Louise to her father at breakfast. 'I can lend her plenty of music and books.'

M. Rambert shrugged his shoulders and answered nothing.

'Marie used to play well enough eighteen months ago,' said Anna. 'She had a pretty voice too, so probably comes for singing lessons. Mathilde could recommend her a teacher. If Marie could ever sing like Mathilde ——'

'If Marie's voice resembles her mother's,' said M. Rambert breaking his egg, 'I conclude she will *not* sing like Mademoiselle Mathilde.'

'Of course not, Mathilde's voice is divine,' cried Anna enthusiastically.

'The last time I heard it, it was not unlike a sparrow with a bad cold, while your aunt sings like a nightingale.'

Louise and Caroline both laughed, but Anna was so indignant that she dared not trust herself to say another word.

'Papa must have asked aunt to come!' cried the girls, when their father left them. 'He, who used to be so dry and cold about her, and would hardly let us speak of her! What a change! Well, we shall see the result.'

Next day, when Madame de Bresse had settled her family in Rue d'Anjou, she called Marie who was vainly trying to arrange in one small cupboard the contents of two closets and a press, and whose red cheeks and dust-covered hands showed how busy she had been since morning.

'Come, my child, we are nearly in order now; change your dress, and let us go and see your cousins.'

Jeanne begged to come too, having arranged all her lesson-books. 'But, mamma, why were not our cousins waiting to welcome us here last night? Uncle came, and he is much busier than they are.'

'Perhaps they thought we should settle down

better alone,' said Madame de Bresse, as she had said to M. Rambert, when he looked astonished not to find his girls there.

'Caroline has a cold, or I know she would have come,' said Jeanne, as they walked along; and Jeanne, unused to the restraints of Paris streets, had some difficulty in walking soberly, without jumping about, as she did in the garden at Bressuire.

M. Rambert was out, but the girls were at home. Not alone, however; Aline, Mathilde, and Adrienne having come to spend the morning with them, partly through curiosity to see the formidable aunt, and partly to give heart to Anna. As for Louise, she needed no encouragement.

Old Baptiste half-apologised when he admitted Madame de Bresse and her daughters. 'There's a lot of young folks there, Madame; they are doing no harm, I dare say; but I had rather see Mademoiselle Marie and Mademoiselle Jeanne.'

Madame de Bresse smiled, and entered the

drawing-room, where Louise now installed herself of mornings, saying she meant to keep the schoolroom as a refuge against sermons. This arrangement suited Caroline, who was now no longer obliged to carry all her books backwards and forwards to her own room.

When Madame de Bresse entered, all the girls rose; Louise and Anna kissed their aunt and cousins, and begged them to come near the fire. The circle was soon re-formed, and Mademoiselle Lequeux, who considered herself a great authority on points of etiquette and manners, began a conversation with Madame de Bresse, of a kind that she supposed suited to the ignorance and simplicity of a provincial lady. The effect was so droll that Anna, who had a keen sense of the ridiculous, could hardly keep from laughing. In the middle of a condescending description of the sights of Paris, Jeanne, who could not stand it any longer, broke out with a request to see Caroline.

'She is in the school-room at work,' said Louise. 'Shall I take you there?'

'Thank you, I know my way. Don't disturb yourself, you seem so exceedingly busy with your embroidery;' and Jeanne darted off in such wrath that she forgot to shut the door.

Louise rose, and carefully closed it. 'I am not sure that she will know her way; our rooms have been changed of late.'

'Oh! Jeanne could find her way in a wood,' said her mother with imperturbable gravity, and resuming the conversation with Mademoiselle Lequeux. Then, having allowed herself to be instructed on various points, she rose. 'I am now fully acquainted — thanks to this young lady!—with the Parisian news since my visit of last week; so, Louise, I will go home, for I am busy. Say to your father that there will be a cup of tea at his service to-night. Will you come too?'

'Caroline has a cold, and we are engaged at a concert at Madame Lequeux's.'

'I will shortly go and renew my acquaintance with Madame Lequeux; she may not quite have forgotten me in spite of my eight years' absence. I should not wish to pay her my first visit only as your chaperon. Mademoiselle Lequeux will have the goodness, perhaps, to convey my message? Adieu, young ladies; adieu, my dear children.'

And Madame de Bresse departed with the manners of a lady quite at her ease, both in her brother-in-law's house and in general society, leaving her nieces and their companions slightly confounded. Louise turned over in her mind her aunt's frank declaration of the part she meant to act towards them as chaperon; Anna felt a secret remorse at the coldness she had shown to Marie; and the three friends could not conceal their surprise at the yet unfaded beauty, the grace of manner, and perfect good-breeding of the country aunt. Aline even remarked that her black velvet bonnet was charming, her dress and mantle of an elegant cut, and that Marie's sleeves were very well embroidered.

'Very presentable relations,' said she aloud. 'I can't see why you should have been so vexed at their arrival. I thought they would have been dressed up like scarecrows, instead of which I am half-inclined to send my next dress to be made up at Coulomniers.'

'My aunt is not a provincial born,' said Louise impatiently. 'And she always lived in Paris, though in a different circle to mamma's, on account of my uncle's religion. All that I dread are her sermons and her sharp eyes. We shall no longer have our little quiet gossips here in peace.'

'Well, you received her coldly enough,' said Mathilde. 'When I am an aunt, I shall expect my nieces to treat me a little better. Your cousins were quite indignant, I saw.'

'Nonsense,' cried Adrienne. 'It was best to let them understand that Louise wants neither a chaperon nor a spy. Why can't the aunt stay at home at Brie, or wherever it is?'

Louise began to feel very cross. The rebuke of one girl, and the commendation of the other, alike proved that her manners had not displayed the exquisite politeness, respectful yet frigid, which she had meant to show to her aunt.

'I shall be much obliged to you, my dear friends,' said she drily, 'if you will speak of something else, and allow us to arrange our family affairs as we choose.'

'Not at all,' gaily replied Aline. 'I came on purpose to see "my aunt," and now that I have the prospect of seeing her again at home, I will disappear. Miss Brown and the carriage are at the door.'

Anna and Mathilde went to the piano without further discussion of the matter, and Adrienne gave Louise a lesson in Russian embroidery.

Meantime Madame de Bresse and Marie went on to the schoolroom. Marie's eyes were glittering with anger, but her mother only smiled.

'Be content, child; this will not last.'

'I hope not, mamma, or I shall have to tell Louise some unpleasant truths.'

'Keep them for your own benefit, my darling,' was the laughing reply as they went into the schoolroom.

There Marie had nothing to be indignant at or to blame. Caroline, who sat by Jeanne with her head on her shoulder, at sight of her aunt burst into a scream of joy, and sprang into her arms, where she lay so long that Marie had to pull her out by her hair, and found that poor little Caroline was crying.

'Oh! it felt as if mamma had come back again,' sobbed she.

CHAPTER XVII.

IN THE PARIS WORLD.

NEXT day, in the afternoon, Madame de Bresse returned to Rue St. Honoré. Her nieces were out shopping; Arthur with them, in spite of his horror of ribbons and counters.

'There is no chance of ever seeing you at home,' explained he to Anna. 'You are always with your friends, or strumming the piano; though the things you play are not half so good as the old tunes you used to sing before you learnt properly. I don't know Italian, and you sing nothing else, which tires out my patience. I like to understand what you are saying.'

'I will learn French opera airs, then.'

'No, I hate operas. But we shall get some good music now, for we shall hear Aunt Cecile. And Marie, too, has a very pretty voice.'

'Prettier than mine, no doubt,' replied Anna, a little offended.

'I never said so; but you see she has had Aunt Cecile for her teacher.'

'Who is of course superior to all the singing-masters in Paris.'

'Probably, because she takes more pains. Capital idea that! of uncle's spending the winter here. I shall get Amedée every Sunday, and Raoul too, whom I like quite as much. He is up to all sorts of fun, in spite of his seriousness; only, when he thinks you are coaxing him to go wrong, you might cut him in little pieces before he'd give in to you. Such a cousin is uncommonly convenient, keeps one all right, and saves one the trouble of having a conscience.'

'Oh, Arthur! I am sure you have a conscience.

'I wish I were as sure! No, no; Raoul wouldn't read his lesson over his neighbour's shoulder, as somebody else does.'

'Of course that isn't right, but everybody does it, you tell me.'

'Except Raoul. Never mind what I say. Only it's jolly to get them, and aunt, and the two girls. Uncle is jolly too, if one could only drag him out of his books. And then how convenient for you and Louise to have a lady to go out with of evenings, instead of that Madame Lequeux whom you're always hooking on to.'

'Madame Lequeux is very kind to us,' said Anna, warmly.

'I dare say. And the garden at Leucelles is uncommonly nice. But for all that she's terribly, terribly vulgar.'

Happily for fraternal harmony they were just entering a shop. Arthur, pulling a wry face, prepared to follow his sister, but at this moment he saw across the street one of his companions, who made signs to him, and, with the briefest possible adieu to Anna, he was off.

She, vexed to find her favourite brother disagreeing with her, and above all for not having been able to explain why her aunt's arrival in Paris was unpleasantly malapropos to herself and Louise—was so disturbed in her mind and so absent, even in choosing a dress, that her sister began making fun of her.

'This pink tarlatan over our old silks would be charming,' mused Louise. 'And Madame Lampen can put a bit of black lace over each flounce, which will give quite a Spanish effect.'

'But are we not nearly out of money?' timidly suggested Anna, though she usually left all financial arrangements to Louse.

'Quite out, but that does not matter; we

shall receive our allowance on the first of January; pay the most pressing of the people, and get out of debt with the rest by degrees.'

This consoling assurance sufficed to the indolent Anna, and the two girls went home. Caroline told them how their aunt and Jeanne had come in their absence, and how she thought aunt was going to pay visits, for she looked so elegant.

'Besides, I think I saw papa give her mamma's visiting-book,' added the child.

'Then we are at peace for to-day,' said Louise, with great relief, as she set to work unpicking the pink silk dresses; whilst Anna, whose vanity and affectionateness were equally wounded by the thought that it was to her aunt and Marie that Arthur looked for good music, went to the piano, and began trying over the airs in La Dame Blanche.

At half-past five a carriage was heard to stop at the door.

'It is aunt, I declare!' cried Anna, flattening her nose against the window. 'She will be wanting to know what we are doing with ourselves this evening.'

'Nothing, luckily; at least we are only going to Madame Lequeux, you know. And we shall not want aunt with us there, I hope.'

'Don't be too sure of that,' said Anna.

Madame de Bresse entered gaily. 'Well, children, I have been paying about twenty visits, and have received ten invitations at least. Will you come to-night to Madame Lequeux's, or to Madame de Barillon's? Choose. I can take Anna with me to the latter; it is a party of young girls.'

Now Madame de Barillon was a charming person, rich, clever, who delighted in giving splendid parties. Aline Lequeux would have given her eyes to go to them, but was never asked; this consideration determined Louise at once.

'We will go to Madame de Barillon's, aunt, if you like,' said she.

'Very well. And now as to your toilette? Have you any white dresses?'

'One of crape and one of tarlatan.'

'What, each of you! The tarlatan then. Ribbons or coral in your hair, no flowers; it is a small party. I will call for you at ten precisely.'

'And Marie?' inquired Anna, secretly wondering where all the expected sermonising was gone to.

'I have promised Marie to let her do just what she likes, and she prefers going to bed to going to a party,' said Madame de Bresse, laughing. 'Adieu now, girls, till evening.'

When their aunt was gone, Louise and Anna stood looking at one another in silent amaze.

'I never saw anything like it,' cried Louise, at last.

'To think,' said Anna, 'that aunt gets us the

entrée to houses where but for her we should have never been asked; and fidgets about our dresses and our hair besides!'

'Oh! I shall stop that; I know what to wear as well as she does, and I don't like being meddled with.'

'She did not meddle; she only asked what dresses we had,' said Anna. 'And I mean to enjoy myself very much at Madame de Barillon's.'

Louise thought the same, and something else, too, which she did not explain to Anna. Evidently her aunt considered the difference in age between her and her sister too great to be set aside; consequently all the grand dissipations—balls, concerts, and so on—would be for herself alone, while Anna would only be taken to young people's entertainments.

Full of this new idea, and very proud of her eighteen years, Louise went to attire herself for the evening. Crossing the schoolroom she perceived Arthur, who had come in for a chat with Caroline.

'She is so kind, just like mamma,' said the little girl. 'She asked me a heap of questions about my health, my lessons, and about you too. Then she spoke of mamma, and then she asked me if I ever thought of God, with whom mamma was, now? And I am afraid I don't, Arthur.'

'Nor I neither,' said Arthur softly, trying to comfort his little sister, who was nearly crying, 'but that is because nobody ever talks to us about Him. If I got such nice letters as Amedée gets from his mother every week; but things will be better now aunt is come.'

Louise shut the door sharply.

'Oh! aunt has been preaching here,' she said to herself. 'Never mind. Caroline may lecture, and Arthur too, as much as ever they like, so as I am left at peace.' And she plunged back into her ribbons.

At ten Madame de Bresse was at the door. A servant came to summon the girls, and the carriage was all in darkness. But when they arrived at Madame de Barillon's, and their aunt removed her cloak, Louise and Anna were astonished at the elegance of her appearance. Simple as her toilette was, the noble grace of her mien made it seem in the best of taste— quite beautiful. Louise gave Anna a nod of satisfaction.

Meantime their aunt arranged carefully the folds of the girls' dresses and the ribbons in their hair; then bade them follow her.

They entered a reception-room far less gilded and decorated than that of Madame Lequeux, but adorned with rare flowers, and hung with valuable pictures. It was half filled with a number of young girls, not one of whom did Louise and Anna know. However, having presented them to their hostess, Madame de Bresse soon made them acquainted with other people.

They talked, they laughed, they danced the polka; they even found themselves engaged for country dances, and enjoying them too. The evening passed charmingly, and, when the carriage came, the two girls owned they had been very much amused, and were sorry to leave, though it was twelve o'clock.

'I am of Cinderella's mind,' said Madame de Bresse. 'I always like to be home by midnight. Who knows what might happen if we stayed later; these fine laces of mine might all be turned into spider-webs.'

'What a pity that would be!' laughed Louise, on whom her aunt's beautiful old point-lace had made a great impression.

'I see you appreciate my mother's finery, which, after lying by twenty years, I find just in the fashion. But here you are at home. Good-night, my children.'

'Nothing to complain of,' said Madame de Bresse, smiling, to her husband, when she came home. 'All was right. Perhaps a strange house and my presence went for something in keeping them in order, poor children! And my toilette has evidently deeply impressed Louise. A good beginning, anyhow.'

CHAPTER XVIII.

DIFFICULTIES RISE.

 GOOD beginning is a good thing, but not everything, as Madame de Bresse soon proved.

At Madame de Barillon's, surrounded by strange faces, and separated from the friends with whom they were accustomed to chatter nonsense, Louise and Anna had recovered their natural girlish reserve, and the good manners which they would doubtless have had, had their mother lived. But when, accepting the numerous invitations of Madame Lequeux, their aunt took them to that lady's house, this true gentlewoman of the old school was a good deal shocked by what she saw; the whisperings, the grimaces, the bursts of rude and loud laughter, and the general line of conduct which some young ladies of the present day think it not unlady-like to indulge in. However, it was a small social party, and Madame de Bresse, thinking that in a larger circle her nieces would be more self-restrained, and also not liking to vex them if she could avoid it, took no notice, either to them or to their father, of what nevertheless pained her very much.

Some days after this Madame Lequeux gave a grand ball. Her aunt considered Anna too young to go; but M. Rambert, rather perplexed, explained that Madame Lequeux had written him a special note, entreating him not to yield to his sister-in-law, and so spoil the pleasure of his daughters.

'You see I could not refuse,' said he.

M. de Bresse, who happened to be present, involuntarily smiled.

'You would have refused, of course?' said M. Rambert sharply.

'Yes, I would; and so have cut short all other similar requests.'

'They will not be made again,' said M. Rambert, so crossly that his brother-in-law did not venture another smile.

The day of the ball arrived. All the week, Madame de Bresse, who by including Marie in their lessons, had come to form some notion of how her nieces' studies were progressing, had gone through a considerable ordeal in the endless complaints of the masters. Exercises were never ready, lessons never learnt; the teachers were half-inclined to give up their pupils in despair. Marie felt almost ashamed of her own superior merits; her work was always conscientious and careful, and sometimes very good. Poor Marie! every day she went home, convinced that she had better stop at home, studying hard herself, and praying for her cousins, who seemed to her to be going straight to perdition. Madame de Bresse was much troubled about her nieces, but, being wiser than Marie, was not so hopeless. She knew that the love of the world and its vanities gradually dies out in many an honest heart; and the love of dress is often replaced by better things. So, on the morning of the ball, she went to Rue St. Honoré, and carefully examined the pink tarlatan dresses and the wreaths of natural flowers which she had ordered for 'her two daughters,' as she often called the motherless girls, somewhat to Marie's indignation. But good Marie kept the bad feeling to herself, and fought against it as much as she could.

As Madame de Bresse stood folding up the pretty gloves she had brought for her nieces, she turned towards Louise to embrace her, saying gently, 'Be happy, my child, as happy as possible, only in moderation. Remember, one does not dance all one's life long.'

Louise, turning round, was much astonished to see tears in her aunt's eyes.

'You are too good to us, aunt,' said she, somewhat touched. 'How this gay life must tire you!'

'Not much; and then it is so pleasant to me to think that I can in any way replace your mother. If only you would sometimes think of other things than the present.'

'Oh, I do, aunt; I think of a great many other things,' answered Louise laughing, and wishing to stop the conversation. Soon afterwards Madame de Bresse went away.

'I know well enough one doesn't dance all one's life long,' said Louise to herself, as she went up to her room; 'the more reason that I should dance while I can, and enjoy myself while I am young. Time enough to be grave when one is old.'

Poor Louise! how did she know she would ever live to be old?

The girls wished to be at the ball early, so as not to lose any of its delights. Consequently, when at ten o'clock, Monsieur and Madame de Bresse, M. Rambert and his daughters were announced, they found some guests already there. Aline came forward and carried off her two friends to a small drawing-room, where she had, she said, established her special quarters; for a while Madame de Bresse remained there too, listening in her secluded corner, to the loud bursts of laughter which the group of young girls indulged in; but, when dancing began, she called her nieces.

Aline resisted. 'Oh, Madame de Bresse, we will stay here,' said she decidedly; 'I have told all the gentlemen, when they want partners, to come and look for us.'

'And the mothers,' said Madame de Bresse, smiling.

'No, we don't want our mothers; they can stop away. We mean to dance all the evening, and promenade between whiles.'

Madame de Bresse looked at Aline, who looked at her in turn, half-obstinately, half-perplexed.

'My brother-in-law has given his daughters to my care; he will think he has lost us all if we stay here. Come, my children.'

Taking Anna's arm she quietly moved away, leaving Louise to follow with as good grace as she might.

That was not saying much; for she and the other young girls had planned to enjoy themselves in full liberty to-night, and Louise would not be beaten. After the first waltz, she composedly rose and crossed the room, full of dancers as it was, alone, to the side of Adrienne Levasseur. Madame de Bresse watched her, and then asked her husband to go and bring Louise quietly back to her side.'

'What, has she strayed so far from her chaperon?'

'Never mind that; you see ever so many other girls are doing the same.'

M. Bresse shrugged his shoulders; young girls were not like this in his time. He did as he was told, and brought his niece back. She sat down beside her aunt with flashing eyes.

'My partner will certainly not know where to find me,' said she.

'Possibly; but, in my younger days, young girls used to stay beside their mothers, which appears to me an excellent custom still.'

'Oh! we girls go where we like now-a-days, English fashion.'

'I doubt if well-brought up English girls go running about ball-rooms quite alone. And, besides, society there is constituted differently from ours. Here is your partner. Anna is already gone away with hers. Now for the dancing, my child.'

Louise, half-shamed by her aunt's exceeding

good-humour, made no reply, and the waltz being done, came back to her side. Anna did the same.

'The aunt is triumphing,' said Aline to Adrienne, as they passed one another with their several partners.

'What aunt?' asked one of the gentlemen.

'An aunt who has come up from the country expressly to prevent one of my young friends from enjoying herself, and who makes her to stick to her side between the dances, and never stir an inch.'

'I should like to make the old lady's acquaintance; she must be just like some aunts of mine,' said the gentleman, laughing.

'Oh! it's all up for to-night, I fear,' said Adrienne. 'But Louise is not quite done for. You should have seen her eyes flash when she was fetched away from here.'

In truth, Louise had not yet laid down her arms. She felt as if the day of battle were come, and, if she allowed her aunt to conquer, liberty would be lost for ever.

At two o'clock in the morning, Madame de Bresse, who for this time only had agreed to renounce her Cinderella custom of retiring at midnight, touched the girls lightly on the shoulder.

'Come, children, we must go home. Your father says he has had enough of the ball.'

Louise rose without saying a word, followed her aunt, and allowed her to wrap her carefully in her cloak; then leaned back, still silent, in the carriage; bade a brief good-night to all, and disappeared to her chamber without stopping to speak even to Anna, who slept with Caroline. Quite tired out, she went to bed and slept; but her mind was made up what to do.

Next morning all looked wearied, except Caroline. Breakfast passed almost in total silence; until, as they were rising, Louise resolutely addressed her father.

'Papa, why does aunt stop me in doing things which all other girls do, and which you have never forbidden?'

It was a clever attack, but M. Rambert, absent as he usually was, had had his eyes opened the night before on the subject of his girls.

'What is it that your aunt hinders you from doing?'

Louise detailed her wrongs, but could get no other reply than that her aunt was quite right.

'Well, papa, if tyranny pleases you, I have no more to say.'

'Tyranny does not please me, nor does impertinence,' said the father sharply. 'I wish you to obey your aunt as if she were myself.' And he went back into his study.

Louise was furious. She reddened and paled alternately. 'She shall pay for this—she shall pay for this!' were all the words that escaped her.

Little Caroline, much perplexed, went up to embrace her sister.

'Get away!' cried Louise, angrily. 'You flatter and coax, and are allowed to do just what you please; but I am mistress here, and I shall go and come as I choose. And if aunt puts spies on my movements, I won't stir from home.'

'That is just what aunt and all of us desire,' cried Caroline, more angrily than truthfully, as she ran back to her grand haven of shelter, the schoolroom, now almost wholly her own domain.

When Madame de Bresse came to be present at the three cousins' singing lesson, she found Louise with eyes so red and swollen, that she thought she had caught cold last night. But, on a sign from Marie, she said nothing, and took no notice of Louise's innumerable false notes—sung half through irritation, and half because she was on the very point of crying. At last the singing mistress could bear it no longer.

'Mademoiselle Louise, you must either sing in tune, or not sing at all; you are putting the two others all wrong.'

Madame de Bresse came to the rescue, apologised for her niece, as being out late last night, told her to sit down and rest, and would not listen to one word of the explanations and revelations of Caroline.

'Aunt ought to be delighted; she has made me cry,' said Louise, bitterly.

But the aunt only said, 'Poor child!' and longed all the more to find the road to her heart.

CHAPTER XIX.

DEBTS AND DANGER.

IN spite of herself, Louise could not manage to pick a quarrel with her aunt, who met her impertinences with unwearied patience, and returned her rudeness and coldness with an anxious and thoughtful tenderness which never failed. Open warfare was impossible. Besides, Anna was already half-conquered, and had ceased to regard her aunt as the common enemy. But for the quizzing and malicious questionings of her companions, Louise herself might have wavered in this opinion, but one word from Aline Lequeux destroyed a week's kindness and patience on the part of Madame de Bresse.

Thus, when they met one day in the street: 'Ah! you are without your watch-dog,' said Aline. 'Come in to us for a minute or so, while Cerberus sleeps.' And then, all Louise's sense of injury returned, and all her indignation. She felt herself an oppressed and tormented creature, and never thought whether Marie, who was under the same care, felt the same; or if, had her own mother been alive, she would have rendered to her the same obedience that was exacted by her aunt.

Meanwhile, poor Louise's secret cares were increasing daily. To avoid the difficulty of paying ready money for materials, she had for some time had all her dresses from the dressmaker, which augmented her bills frightfully. And, unconsciously, Madame de Bresse had increased her nieces' difficulties. One day, shocked to see the darned condition of Louise's stockings, she had gone over the girls' wardrobe, and advised the buying of a few new under-clothes, which had to be paid for at once. This sum, small as it was, and the money that had from time to time to be dispensed, just to quiet creditors, still further crippled their resources. For ever so long, Caroline had been clad entirely in her sisters' old clothes—a proceeding against which she sometimes revolted, declaring that she had a third share in the allowance, and ought now and then to have the privilege of buying something quite new.

But Louise had succeeded in convincing herself, and half convincing Anna, that their income need not be equally divided, since the third sister, never going out at all, did not require elegant clothes. Nevertheless, once a year she was obliged to give Caroline a really new frock, which still further impoverished the hapless purse.

'Who makes your bonnets, Marie?' Louise

asked one day, seeing a very pretty one that had been just sent home.

'Mamma orders them; she says I have no taste at all,' replied Marie, laughing. 'I believe this one comes from Mademoiselle Blondot.'

'Then I will go to her; I am not satisfied with our milliner.'

'I think your bonnets are very pretty,' said Marie, carelessly: the subject did not interest her much. She soon resumed her discussion with Anna; upon an English book they had both been reading, and which interested them much.

'Only I should like a few more events in it,' said Anna.

Marie liked it precisely because it had no events—was just every-day life, where the people tried hard to do right, and never succeeded, yet were always trying again. 'It seems to me as if I knew them all,' said Marie, sighing.

'Oh! I dipped into the book,' Louise said, 'but I found it far too serious. All the people in it are so very discontented with themselves, and the most amiable of them is laid up for six months on a sofa. I like more cheerful stories. And then I have not worked at English as Marie has; I find it too hard to read to enjoy it much.'

And so she went away, to put in execution a brilliant plan.

She dared not order new bonnets from her own milliner, whose unpaid account was so alarming that she had hid it in the farthest corner of her desk, so as to see it no more. But she might try her aunt's milliner, to whose shop she had often been with Madame de Bresse.

Mademoiselle Blondot, delighted to get new customers, promised to make for Mademoiselle Rambert three pink bonnets, at a price so reasonable that Louise was quite astonished; not considering that she was being charged the same as her aunt, who always paid ready money;

Mademoiselle Blondot little guessing how long she would have to wait for hers.

At the week's end the bonnets arrived, and appeared next Sunday at church. Marie, who was always afraid of wearing new things on a Sunday, lest she should think too much about them, was greatly scandalised at the splendour of her cousins' appearance.

'People will stare at you in church,' she whispered to her chief ally, Caroline.

'Let them stare then. It's their blame.'

'But we ought not to help other people to do wrong,' persisted Marie.

'I don't care! I'll take off my bonnet if you like; but as Louise and Anna won't take off theirs, you had better shut your eyes and fancy we have our old bonnets on. It's all the same.'

Marie followed this prudent advice, but nevertheless, evil was at hand.

One of the young workwomen of the milliner to whom the girls owed so much money, met in

'What is this, Louise? Six hundred francs owed to Madame Valeureux in two years? . . . What on earth have you been doing with your allowance?'

Page 229.

the Rue St.-Honoré the whole family going to church. She recognised Louise, Anna, and Caroline; but she did not recognise the pink bonnets.

'Ah! they are bought elsewhere than at our shop,' thought she to herself, and determined at once to inform Madame Valeureux.

Louise, delighted equally with her new bonnet and her scheme for obtaining it, was utterly unaware of the storm that was brewing over her head, when one day her father walked into the school-room with a bill in his hand.

'What is this, Louise? Six hundred francs owed to Madame Valeureux in two years? Since your first mourning bonnets, nothing paid for? What on earth have you been doing with your allowance?'

Louise stood stupified. 'It is those horrid pink bonnets,' she thought to herself; 'but how could Madame Valeureux find all out?' Then she said, terribly frightened, 'Please, papa, we have never had enough money—and—and—it was impossible to pay for everything.'

'If so, would it not have been common honesty to tell me the fact?' said her father in extreme anger. 'And meantime, you ought to have been careful. Who knows how much more you may have been spending? I must enquire into the matter immediately.'

And he went out, leaving his daughters in a state of consternation indescribable.

This was only the beginning of troubles. It seemed as if, once given the hint, every shop where the girls had dealt was down upon them. The dressmaker, whose account was still more dreadful than the milliner's, the bootmaker, the glover, the perfumer, all sent in their bills addressed to M. Rambert. He ticketed them, tied them up in a bundle, and sent for his daughters.

'Look here,' said he, 'your bills come to two thousand five hundred francs, your whole year's allowance; therefore I shall cease giving it. You have proved yourselves unfitted to be trusted with so large a sum; therefore I shall consult your aunt as to how your real wants are to be provided for in future.'

Poor absent-minded M. Rambert had never managed his daughters worse. The wrath of Louise broke out without bounds.

'I would rather not buy a single new riband for a year to come than buy it under the direction of my aunt.'

'Then don't buy it at all, which will be infinitely more economical for me,' said her father drily. 'Meantime, I will pay these bills, desiring the tradespeople to supply you with nothing further except for ready money.'

Even the indolent Anna was roused at last. When the three girls, at an imperative gesture from their father, left him and went to their own room, she was as furious as Louise; she walked to and fro in great indignation.

'I knew it was wrong to run into debt,' said she, 'but to desire the tradesmen not to supply us! It is an open disgrace, a thing intolerable! Why does not papa give us enough money?'

'He might have done so,' said Caroline, 'if we had been more reasonable in our expenses.'

'You, poor little thing!' said Anna, touched by a sentiment of justice. 'Why, *you* have been reasonable enough. Eight hundred francs will more than cover all that has been spent upon you.'

'And papa has often given us money,' timidly added Caroline.

Anna's wrath returned. 'Yes, just for a whim, but not enough to be of any real use to us. But, Louise, you say nothing. What are you thinking about?'

'I was thinking,' said Louise slowly, 'that we shall have to go to Madame Lequeux's tradesmen. They have not been forbidden to supply us.'

Her sister's coolness rather shocked Anna. 'I forewarn you, Louise; I won't run into debt again.'

'Nor I, if I can help it.' And Louise began to examine her wardrobe.

M. Rambert, thoroughly unhappy and perplexed, went to his sister-in-law, to whom he had as yet said nothing of this unpleasant affair. When he had told it, Madame de Bresse could with difficulty abstain from saying what she felt —how badly he had managed, how he had just taken the certain means to irritate his daughters, without making them in the least see their errors. However, she contented herself with entreating him to say nothing more to the tradespeople beyond paying their bills.

'Otherwise,' said she, 'your daughters' credit will suffer. Be content; I will persuade them to go to tradesmen whom I know.'

'But I have stopped their allowance, and I

wanted to consult you about the manner of providing them with what they really require.'

'If you ask my advice, I say, continue their allowance as before; only deduct from it something periodically, till their debts are cleared, and insist, for the future, that they should show you their monthly bills. With care, and a wardrobe as well supplied as theirs is now, I think they might do, for this year, with two thousand francs. By and by you will have to increase the sum, meanwhile a little present now and then will help them on. What is most to be avoided is debt; with no allowance, this is sure to happen. Be tender to them, and be just also.'

M. Rambert consented; telling his daughters frankly that they owed his change of mind to the wise counsels of their aunt.

Outraged and indignant as she was, Louise accepted the compromise, and remembering the pretty pink bonnets, reconciled herself to be supplied by her aunt's tradespeople, and moreover, advised by her aunt, in the matter so very near her heart—her toilette.

CHAPTER XX.

THE CRISIS.

IT was already April when this financial crisis of the young Mesdemoiselles Rambert occurred. Previously, some lady had hinted to their father that the sum he gave them could not possibly suffice for such elegant toilettes as theirs; but he, accustomed, when he thought of it at all, to compare his daughters' appearance with that of Aline Lequeux or Mathilde Labrousse, had had no idea of the real state of things, until his sister-in-law's arrival. Then, seeing Marie, his niece, so simply dressed, he began to concern himself about his daughters.

'Oh, Louise and Anna can afford to be more elegant than Marie,' said Madame de Bresse. 'There are three of them, and Caroline spends almost nothing. Besides, Marie spends so much upon her poor people.'

M. Rambert sighed. His daughters never thought of the poor. In his new intimacy with his late wife's kindred, he often found Marie not only more reasonable, but gayer and pleasanter than his own girls. When he saw her throw aside her work to execute a commission for her mother, sing for an hour, without being asked, the German music of which her father was so fond, and let her own tasks slip by in order to help Jeanne in hers, M. Rambert sometimes wished that Louise and Anna were less eagerly occupied with frivolities. He even began to consider whether piety was not a good thing—for women; and that even the strong stern faith of M. de

Bresse was excusable, considering the good effects it apparently produced on his family.

Spring arrived, and Marie, taking a run over to Bressuire with her father, came back with her hands full of anemones, intoxicated with the odour of early violets, and more sick than ever of Paris, where there was no rest, she declared, not even at church.

Her mother spoke less strongly, but even she felt that this had been a winter lost. She had gained so little of the affection of her nieces, had had so few chances of serious talk with them, and they had still such a dread of her, that she was inclined to overlook the evil she had actually prevented, in regretting the good left undone.

M. de Bresse was more patient, and better satisfied. Coming to Paris simply to fulfil a disagreeable duty, with little hope of effecting any real good, he had seen his relations with his brother-in-law gradually change to pleasant intimacy, and the influence of his wife gradually increase. Also, his translation of the Psalms advanced: he had met various learned Hebraists, and had had time to begin, among the Paris poor, various benevolent schemes connected with his own strong religious convictions, which interested him so much that he was in no haste to leave them.

But Madame de Bresse longed for home, and Louise, though growing accustomed to her aunt's care, began to think with pleasure that soon there would be nobody to trouble themselves about how she passed her mornings—when one morning, after a joyful exclamation from Jeanne of how soon she would revisit her dear chickens at Bressuire, M. Rambert turned anxiously to his sister-in-law.

'You are not going home?' said he, looking quite alarmed.

'We must, my dear Louis; my girls are

thirsting for fresh air, and so am I. Charles alone seems indifferent to it.'

'Because he sees how impossible it is for me to spare you.'

'Or else, because he has found his true vocation, and turned missionary. He is perfectly happy from morning till night in the garrets of the Rue St.-Antoine. Even his beloved Hebrew fades before the delight of this new avocation.'

'But, Cécile, you have a mission too—taking care of my daughters,' said M. Rambert, rather impatiently.

'Send them to me at Bressuire, and I will fulfil it.'

M. Rambert hesitated. 'I have another plan, but I know not how you will like it, you have such a determined air.'

Madame de Bresse here sent her girls out of the room, as their uncle did not seem to like speaking before them.

'Thank you, Cécile,' said he, 'it was to leave you free that I did not wish your daughters to hear my plan, for I am sure they will be disappointed if you decline it. I wanted you to take all our girls to Switzerland and Germany, and the boys to join us in the holidays.'

'Then you will accompany us?' asked Madame de Bresse, much surprised, for she had never known her brother-in-law quit Paris for more than two days together.

'Yes, perhaps; I want a little relaxation.'

'But you will weary so if you have nothing to do?'

'And I have no missionary vocation,' said M. Rambert, laughing.

'I think not,' was the grave reply; 'for what could you say to the poor folks?'

Her sweet but penetrating look, and the gentle conviction in her words which implied that *she* would have something to say to the poor and the sorrowful, made a certain impression on M. Rambert. He remained silent for a little; then asked, 'And my travelling plan; what say you to it?'

'I must consider, and talk with Charles. For myself, I hesitate much; I doubt even if we ought to return to Paris next winter. Louise is so on her guard against me, that I feel I do her no good.'

'Do you not see that even being on her guard, as you see, is an advantage? it a little hinders her from yielding to the torrent that might sweep her away. I know very well my poor child is very ungrateful to you; some day she may know your goodness and be thankful for it.'

'Do not speak of gratitude,' said Madame de Bresse, much moved. 'I am only too happy that you allow me a little to fill their mother's place to your girls.'

When her brother-in-law departed, Madame de Bresse was unwillingly vanquished a second time. Great was the sacrifice she was making in exchanging a quiet summer at Bressuire to scour mountains and forests with five young girls, who would be often tired out, often in bad humour, and always inclined to run about when their mother longed to rest.

Personally Madame de Bresse disliked travelling very much. Brought up in Paris in the midst of a brilliant society, the serious half of her character had not developed until after her marriage, when she had the constant company of a pious, learned, and distinguished man. Then, she cared not to travel. Except once to England, and once to Belgium, during twenty years she had never been out of France. It was a little late, at forty years of age, to begin journeying about the world. But then she felt that once clear out of Paris life, the many difficulties which had arisen from the totally different views of the aunt and the nieces on this subject, would lighten; that when Louise was removed from the influence of her frivolous companions, and associated constantly with Marie, whose reserved nature required time and opportunity to have any influence at all, it was just possible that both she and Anna might open their hearts to the affection which they now repulsed.

Filled with these thoughts, and her heart brimming over with tenderness for the motherless children, Madame de Bresse rose to summon her daughters. Jeanne looked anxiously at her—it was so seldom that at Bressuire the children were sent out of the room when business matters were discussed. Marie herself — the sensible Marie—was a little disturbed. The beginning of the conversation had seemed to threaten the peace of that quiet summer at home, and she was already up in arms against any plan which carried her away from Bressuire. To stay in Paris, or to live as a double household in some country place just outside Paris, would have been odious to her, and her mother's visible perplexity augured ill. Respect held Marie's tongue fast, but she was not sorry when Jeanne spoke out.

'What was this mysterious secret that uncle wanted to tell you, mamma?'

Madame de Bresse laughed. 'My sending you away that you might not hear it, is a reason why I should not tell you the secret now. But never mind! it is no secret, the mystery is over.'

Jeanne, a little confused, began some curious speculations concerning the word 'now,' whilst Marie, more and more surprised, gathered up the sewing which her sister had thrown down, folded her own, and quietly went to fetch Macaulay's 'History of England,' which she was reading aloud to her mother.

That evening Madame de Bresse waited for her husband more anxiously than usual. She wanted his decision to guide hers. Her perplexed conscience kept pulling her sometimes to the right, sometimes to the left; picturing on one hand the neglected poor and village school at Bressuire, on the other her nieces passing the summer at Leucelles, or going to the sea-side with Madame Levasseur.

As usual, when especially expected, M. de Bresse came in later than his wont. When his wife ran to open the door for him, she saw his face was graver than ordinary, though serene.

'You are back at last,' she said. 'I thought you would never come at all to-day.'

'I thought so too,' and he drew her beside him on the sofa. 'Old Magenan is dead, Cécile.'

'Dead! and how?' cried Madame de Bresse, much troubled.

'While I was with one of his neighbours, I was fetched to him; he had dropped insensible from his chair. I lifted him on his pallet-bed and sent for a doctor; but it was his third attack of apoplexy, and the end was come. He was bled, but no blood flowed. He just opened his eyes, recognised me, and said, loud enough for everybody to hear him, "Jesus!" Then he died.

I spoke a little to those who were about the bed —if I could have made them feel what I felt, not one of them would have left the room an unbeliever.'

He stopped, much moved by what he had witnessed. His wife said, 'Thank God!'—for old Magenan had been one of the souls won by her husband's words and prayers.

'And I am not sure,' she said, 'but there will be another ere long. Louis came this morning, and made to me a most astounding proposition. He wished us all to travel together this summer through Switzerland and Germany.'

'I thought of such a scheme myself, but feared Louis would not consent to put his daughters under the influence of a certain terrible woman of my acquaintance.'

'You think of lots of things which you never tell to me, Charles; but I have no time to quarrel with you. Say what you think of the plan.'

'I find it excellent, of course, being half my own, and only wanting Louis's consent.'

'And mine.'

'Oh! you will begin by objecting, and end by coming round to my opinion. As *you* know, I think you have got farther into your nieces' hearts than you suspect. Once away from milliners' shops, and face to face with mountains, they will listen, and you will speak, much more freely and satisfactorily.'

'And Bressuire?'

'Luckily I am not a farmer. And besides, the things will grow without my being there to see. If my bailiff makes mistakes, it is his fault, not mine.'

'And my poor people? And my school? Who will take care of these things?'

'Martha. We cannot carry her with us, good soul! Catherine will be enough, and we can send our Martha home to nurse the sick and spoil the babies in the village, which is the real delight of her life. It is only through charity and affection that she condescends to be your waiting-maid.'

Madame de Bresse laughed. 'Yes, I do believe it is from Martha that Marie has learnt her fondness for taking charge of the poor. What I do from duty, they two do from absolute enjoyment. So all my objections are removed.'

'Except those which concern yourself, and those you never speak of,' said M. de Bresse affectionately. 'You who detest travelling, how shall you endure drifting on from inn to inn?'

'You are so fond of inns that that must console me,' returned she gaily. 'If you give up this summer of work, so must I. Our conference is ended; may God bless the result of it!'

'He will, my love,' said M. de Bresse, as he leaned thoughtfully against the fireplace. 'Our sole aim is to gather souls for Him, and if He sent us in search of them to China or Siberia, I think we should cheerfully go.'

'At present, happily, we need not go quite so far,' said Madame de Bresse gently, for she was touched by the devotedness of her husband; though she felt deeply thankful that Providence did not require her to leave all, and follow him to the world's end. For she had often thought that had she and her husband been childless, he would have wished for a missionary career, and she never would have had strength to carry out the sacrifice.

CHAPTER XXI.

A LONG JOURNEY.

GREAT was the joy in the two households when the children learnt M. Rambert's project. Marie expressed a momentary astonishment that her mother should prefer running about the world, as she called it, instead of returning quietly to Bressuire; but, this over, she did not hide her satisfaction in the plan.

'Since Martha may go and take care of our poor people and our school, I am content. They will be all right, and I can enjoy the mountains. I have read somewhere, that every mountain-top has a little of the glory which shone upon Mount Sinai; is that true, mamma?'

'I cannot tell, my child, for I never saw a mountain; but your father has often told me what a strange emotion affected him when he was on the summit of the Himalayas. He never, he said, felt God nearer than on that day.'

'I wish I could go to the Himalayas!' sighed Marie, whose religious faith was more deep than joyful, and who envied often the profound peace which was written on the countenance of her father.

Less serious reasons caused the delight of Louise and her sisters in the projected tour. They dreaded either spending the summer in Paris, which would be wearisome and not 'genteel,' or else visiting from house to house—a system which began to please them rather less than at first. For Louise had a proud spirit, and she had unfortunately overheard Madame Lequeux say to one of her acquaintances, 'These poor Rambert girls have nobody to look after them, they want amusement terribly, so I have them at our house as often as possible.' Also, she had noticed that Mathilde's mother liked to invite other of her daughter's friends than her dear Anna. Perhaps these two things had softened Louise's heart towards Madame de Bresse. The careless-minded girl began to feel a little of the charm of family ties, and of the affection to which she had an absolute right.

Anna planned much sketching, making a herbal for Mathilde, and hearing German music; but the beauties of nature never affected her much. It was to Caroline that Marie talked of mountains, glaciers, wild or beautiful scenery, such as her father was never weary of describing or she of hearing about.

'Switzerland must have changed much since my last tour, twenty-five years ago,' said he. 'But mountains and glaciers never change—no more than their unchangeable Creator.'

And Marie pressed closer to her father, between whom and herself there was always the most perfect sympathy.

M. Rambert had travelled even less than his sister-in-law, and also had not had the advantage of M. de Bresse for his guide. Consequently, as soon as the matter was settled, he began to accumulate all sorts of necessaries for the journey, each more complicated and more unnecessary than the other—umbrellas which became folding-chairs, and folding-chairs which turned into umbrellas, with the advantage of being satisfactory as neither, and of taking at least twenty minutes to pack and unpack when the transportation was necessary; spy-glasses which required a boy and a man to carry them; travelling-bags containing everything you did not want, and nothing that you did. All these admirable articles were collected in advance. M. de Bresse was much amused with his brother-in-law, and sometimes just a trifle impatient too.

'We shall certainly have forty additional trunks as our travelling impedimenta,' said he to his wife.

'Never mind,' she laughed. 'Catherine and Baptiste will see after them.'

'Catherine and Baptiste! It is clearly seen, my dear, that you have never travelled. Catherine and Baptiste will only be two boxes more, and two people, for me to take charge of! If only Louis would give up Baptiste, I am sure Pierre would quit his little cottage at Gersaint to accompany me once more, and he is first rate as a courier. However, we must leave Louis to manage his own affairs. My comfort is, if we have too many boxes, we shall be sure to lose a few of them on the road.'

Her husband's *sang-froid* so frightened Madame de Bresse, that she gave Marie private orders to count all the boxes on arrival and departure, every day of this formidable tour.

June approached. M. and Madame de Bresse

went to Bressuire to make final arrangements. Marie accompanied them, Jeanne being left with Caroline. After selecting for their summer clothes what should be left and what taken to Switzerland, the mother and daughter still found time to go round and visit their poor people, providing for the needs of some, and saying a kind word to others, whose troubles had greatly accumulated during their long absence from Bressuire.

'Ah! Mademoiselle Martha is very good,' said they all, ' but why could not Madame stay at home here instead of running off first to Paris and then to Switzerland? What is the use of seeing so many countries?'

M. Rambert, on his part, arranged for the three boys to work together at his house under a tutor, who would see them safe off daily to their respective colleges, so that all minds were easy concerning them. And Marie and Anna sympathised more than usual when they began to count the days that would elapse before their brothers were able to join them in Switzerland.

At last, one fine July day, the whole family commenced its journey. It filled a railway-carriage, likewise an entire omnibus, and the excess of luggage to be paid for was so frightful that M. de Bresse again hinted at the execution of his scheme of leaving two or three boxes on the road.

'I must, otherwise we shall pay the value of our goods and chattels twice over,' said he.

They were to sleep at Lyons, and there spend a part of the next day. In all his travelling, M. de Bresse had never been to Lyons, and he wanted to see the silk-mills, where are employed, either singly or in numbers, those weavers who scatter over the world such gorgeous fabrics, while they themselves often live in misery and poverty. Hospitals, too, he desired to visit; and Louise and Anna now entered one for the first time. The long series of beds occupied by pale and worn faces, the atmosphere of sickness and sorrow around, went to the girls' very hearts. They had never thought, poor children, that there were so many unhappy people in the world as they saw here in the hospital of Lyons.

'How sad it is, uncle!' whispered Louise, taking his arm. 'Do let us pass on.'

'It is sad, my dear child, unless we remember that God is beside every bed of pain, strengthening and comforting. How blessed to be His mouthpiece, as it were, and carry His message to each suffering soul!'

Louise regarded M. de Bresse with astonishment. Nobody had ever spoken to her in this way before; and she was so struck by both his words and his look, that she remained silent for at least five minutes—a thing hitherto unheard of with Louise Rambert.

A few more hours' travelling took them to Geneva, where both the brothers-in-law had friends; so they were to stay some days. The lake promised endless excursions. When, next morning, awaking in the hotel, the girls saw that wide blue sheet of water spread out before their eyes, with the amphitheatre of mountains and glaciers beyond, they uttered an irrepressible cry of admiration. For the first time Louise felt towards Marie an instinct of real intimacy: she opened the door which divided their two rooms, and entered, crying out:

'Oh, Marie, how beautiful this is!'

Marie, still in her dressing-gown, was kneeling in front of the window, her eyes fixed on the scene before her, with an expression of such rapt adoration, that Louise stood still, quite silent, as in her talk the evening before with her uncle. There began to dawn upon her the divineness of that faith which sees in everything made the Omnipotent Maker of it all.

'It is so beautiful that it chokes me,' said Marie, slowly rising, and still watching the lake and the mountains. 'How great God is!'

This thought was at the core of all Marie's enjoyment. And she did enjoy herself. She was the most indefatigable in excursions, the most insatiable in mountain-climbing, the most adventurous in expeditions down the lake; but all her pleasures resolved themselves into one ever-present idea—the goodness of God, who had made for man such a beautiful world. Her father, who loved these wanderings as much as Marie, often took her with him, while Louise and Anna, easily fatigued, stayed at Geneva with their aunt. M. de Bresse enjoyed these new sympathies with his daughter all the more because Madame de Bresse, who could not get up their tourist enthusiasm, sometimes laughed at them, sometimes feared for them.

'Let us alone,' said M. de Bresse, much amused. 'Cécile, I recognise my own blood in my daughter's passion for climbing. If you had only known me when I was twenty years old!'

'But Marie never cared to do any climbing at Bressuire,' said the mother.

'The sacred fire was not yet kindled,' returned M. de Bresse, as he departed with his child.

They visited Chamounix, Lausanne, Vevey, Montreux, and had still to drive round the lake of Geneva before passing on to that of Neufchâtel. July was nearly out, and they waited impatiently for news of the boys, whose letters were short and few, the young scholars being absorbed by examination cares. Arthur was far ahead in everything, which made Anna so conceited that she sometimes tormented Marie by comparing him with her brothers. The two girls often disputed over the merits of the respective colleges, but both M. Rambert and M. de Bresse having been educated at the one to which Arthur went, Anna had formidable allies, and Marie generally ended by the pathetic exclamation, 'It isn't my fault, papa, if you *would* send my brothers to Louis-le-Grand.'

No letters arriving, it was decided to continue their excursion; and Madame de Bresse, who much preferred lakes to mountains, voted for Neufchâtel.

'There at least,' she said, 'we can go in a steam-boat, which is less fatiguing than your mountain-passes.'

Anna and Caroline agreed, one through indolence, the other through weakness, she having grown much too fast of late. Therefore, while Marie, Louise, and Jeanne ran about all over the country, these two usually sat and worked beside their aunt; and Anna, always alive to the influence of the moment, began to be interested in many things Madame de Bresse talked about and many books that she read. For Caroline, her great eyes were for ever watching her aunt; she seemed to devour her words, and expressed for her day by day a continually increasing affection.

As for Louise, alone on the mountains with Marie and her uncle—concerning her too the good aunt was hopeful and content.

CHAPTER XXII.

THE CATASTROPHE.

RETURNING from Neufchâtel, in spite of fine weather, lovely scenery, mountains painted in the blue sky, and all the charms of travelling, everybody was glad to be back at Geneva. There they were to find the boys' letters, and learn by telegram what success they had had in the examinations. The affectionate sisters almost forgot lakes and glaciers; they felt themselves now at Paris, at the Sorbonne; and they spoke only of books, and schoolfellows, and the different chances of the three boys. Madame de Bresse spoke little, but felt much; both for her nephew and her sons.

Geneva at last;—and while Madame de Bresse unpacked the travelling-bags, and gave to their sitting-room that nameless air of *inhabitedness* which some people can throw so charmingly around in ever so brief a stay, the girls went to the post-office with M. Rambert and M. de Bresse. There was a mass of letters: two for Madame de Bresse, one for M. Rambert, two for Marie, one for Anna, one for Caroline.

'But what of the boys? give me news of the boys,' cried M. de Bresse with an air of sham despair. 'This is the result of having two sons at Paris: all their letters are for their mother and sisters. Louise, Jeanne, shake hands! We are all companions in misfortune.'

'Raoul thinks he is all right in his Greek translation, and Amédée fancies his Latin verses are not so bad,' cried Marie exultingly. 'Perhaps we shall have a telegram to-morrow.'

'Arthur says he has worked hard, and that it is very hot,' added Anna, skimming over her letter as fast as she could; 'he knows nothing of his chances, but he thinks they are pretty equal. We have come back here just in time; the distribution of prizes takes place to-day.'

'No, to-morrow! Stop—yes, you are right, Anna,' said Marie. 'One doesn't know how the days pass when one is out enjoying oneself. What should we do if it were not for Sunday?'

'Come, let us go back; your mother will be impatient,' said M. de Bresse.

No, Madame de Bresse was not impatient. She stood waiting on the balcony of the hotel with a paper in her hand.

'A telegram!' cried everybody, and never was a mountain climbed more quickly and eagerly than the hotel staircase.

'One first prize, two second prizes, one fourth prize!' called out the mother, quite indifferent to passers-by.

'Who? who?' shouted the girls; while M. Rambert, carefully shutting the door behind him, stretched out a hand for the telegram; but his sister-in-law held it fast.

'Raoul a first, Arthur two second, Amédée a fourth. That is brilliant!'

'Thank God! Our dear children!' murmured M. de Bresse.

'Is it his Greek translation that has brought Raoul such felicity?'

'I am keeping you waiting, Louise, but the news is so good; our boys have well earned their holiday.'

'The crazy fellows,' laughed M. Rambert over the telegram, which ended by an 'Hurrah!' 'I wonder what the telegraph clerk thought of the three young madmen who besieged his office in a body.'

'Perhaps he himself got prizes when he was a lad: let us hope it. And now our boys will be here almost as soon as their letters.'

' I suppose " Friday evening" is a concise way of expressing that they will be here to-night,' said M. de Bresse, when he at last got a sight of the telegram.

' They will not have time,' Anna said. ' Raoul and Arthur will dine to-night with the minister of public instruction, and to-morrow is the distribution of prizes.'

'When poor Amédée will have to stay alone with his tutor,' cried Jeanne sorrowfully.

' Amédée is jealous of no one's pleasure,' said Marie. 'He will make himself quite happy with M. Royer, and they will all soon be here.'

In spite of Anna's prediction, Raoul did find time to write a word to his father, stating their time of departure and probable arrival, with a word or two only about their success the night before.

' My dear son!' murmured the mother as she read them. ' Raoul is safe from all conceit : I only hope Amédée will not have his head turned.'

But Amédée's sisters had, anyhow. They were quite crazy with joy and pride. Louise, less fond of Arthur than Anna was, and less interested in his successes and pleasures, had nevertheless been delighted to see that the cousin of Aline Lequeux, and the brother of Adrienne Levasseur, had not even been named in the examination. This triumph completed her satisfaction, but her good aunt was rather sorry.

At four o'clock they all went in a body to the railway-station. Already Caroline and Jeanne had been tormenting Madame de Bresse for half an hour to let them start, lest they should miss the train's arrival, and the boys might go to the hotel on the top of the omnibus, where the girls could not follow them, and would not be able to welcome them for a full hour. But the little ones were not attended to, which often happened to poor Caroline and Jeanne; and it was as well, for when they arrived the train was still not in.

Shortly, however, they heard its whistle, and it was difficult for the parents to keep their girls within the barrier.

In three bounds the three successful scholars were on the platform, and hugged by their affectionate sisters, the mother calmly waiting her turn.

'Mamma,' said Amédée, 'will you condescend to kiss me without a laurel crown? I thought of borrowing one of those which deck the noble brows of Arthur here, but I reflected that you would not approve of a jay in peacock's feathers.'

'I love you just as you are,' said his mother, and kissed him, in spite of the public.

The two fathers shook hands with their boys, and vanished, partly to see after luggage and partly to get rid of the pathetic scene of kisses. Shortly after, the whole party were in the hotel; Anna and Jeanne clamouring for a sight of the crown and the books.

'We left them in Paris,' said Arthur; 'you

have enough boxes to drag about with you, without one specially for our prizes. We should have had to hire a separate cab to convey them from inn to inn.'

The boys' jokes amused everybody, and did everybody good too; for their fun was that of young people who, having worked hard and well, come out determined to enjoy themselves. The grave Raoul himself laughed as if he were crazy, and made plans of holiday expeditions which would have taken six years instead of six weeks to carry out.

'Now, where shall we begin?' said Amédée. 'We'll not stay here, for you must have seen everything. Shall we go to Berne in the Lesser Cantons?'

'I vote for the Lesser Cantons,' said M. de Bresse; 'there will be fewer tourists. They have spoiled my Switzerland; it is no longer a paradise for happy savages like Marie and me.'

'Since when has Marie become a savage?'

asked Arthur. 'It seems to me she has only grown a trifle prettier.'

Everybody laughed at this double-edged compliment.

'Marie has become a savage, my dear child,' replied M. Rambert, seriously, 'in consequence of being able to keep up with her father in his long walks, and learning to look down precipices without her head swimming.'

'Has Louise made much progress in that art?' asked Raoul.

Louise declared that she had not; that she only walked like ordinary people, and got tired and cross like ordinary people. 'And when we are utterly exhausted, off start my uncle and Marie for a second expedition twice as long and twice as fatiguing as the first one.'

'I'll join them!' cried Amédée. 'When shall we start? My impatience knows no bounds.'

'Will not that sight suffice you for one day?' said the mother, drawing him to the window, where the lake lay sleeping in the moonlight.

'It is superb, mamma! But still, I came bent upon wandering. The lake of the Four Cantons draws me by a force irresistible. I can no longer fight against destiny.'

'You goose! we are to start to-morrow,' said M. Rambert. 'You will soon be upon this lovely lake that you dream of so much.'

'Dream! That reminds me, uncle, I think I rather want sleep. Raoul, Arthur, will you come to bed?'

'By-and-bye,' said Raoul, who was talking in a low voice with his father.

'Then I'm off. Good-night, mamma. Goodnight, everybody.'

Dragging Arthur with him, Amédée disappeared. The mirth of the party disappeared with him. They all found out that they were very tired and had to be up early to-morrow, and took themselves off to bed.

'What are you thinking of, Charles?' said the mother, noticing how happy her husband looked.

'Of Raoul. If he lives, the boy will be to us an infinite joy.' And he told how, amidst all his school-work, the boy had found time to take his father's place in visiting the poor of the Faubourg St. Antoine, and what a noble devotion he had shown there, though from his excessive reserve it had been difficult to find this out.

Next day, at 5 A.M., everyone was stirring; boxes locked, travelling-bags closed, and travelling arrangements enquired into. M. de Bresse allowed his family to enquire; but he himself only smiled—he had no notion of being consigned from inn to inn like a bit of luggage; and he sometimes horrified his wife and his brother-in-law by neglecting all sensible advice on their route, and trusting only to the acuteness which his long travels about the world had given him.

Arrived at the Lake of the Four Cantons, and

settled at the fine hotel there, the party began making expeditions, on foot or on mule-back, up the passes of the mountains. Madame de Bresse at first voluntarily accompanied them; but her strength failed, and she declared she must rest one entire day at the hotel. Louise was foot-sore, in consequence of too thin and too tight boots; Jeanne and Caroline were tired, and Anna was always ready to rest herself.

'I see I shall be the only representative of the feminine half of us to-morrow,' said Marie, laughing. 'Will you come, uncle?'

'Gladly,' said M. Rambert, who was busily engaged carving on his Alpenstock the names of the different places he had visited lately. 'I scarcely know myself; I am become quite a mountaineer.'

Raoul said he would stay with his mother, and take her for a sail down the lake. Amédée and Arthur were delighted to join the expedition. So the whole party left early next morning.

The mother and her eldest son had had two hours of quiet talk, when Louise came in to the sitting-room, saying they could not have their ordinary boatman; he had been caught up by two Englishmen who wished to circumnavigate the lake.

'Then I'll go and find you another,' said Raoul; 'for we must pass an idle day on this blue water.'

He had some difficulty in this, for the boatmen were all engaged over-night; but at length, about one o'clock, Madame de Bresse, her son, and the four girls descended to the shore to embark.

'What a tiny boat it is!' said she, anxiously. 'Don't stir, children, pray!'

Raoul said that he had brought a book which would send Caroline and Jeanne sound asleep in no time, and then they would be safe, all of them.

'No, indeed,' said Jeanne, 'I won't go to

sleep; but I hope I know how to keep quiet, especially in a boat.'

Half-an-hour afterwards they were at the middle of the lake, Raoul reading English poetry to his mother, Caroline knitting, Anna and Louise talking together in an undertone, Jeanne beginning to think it all very tiresome, when all of a sudden she saw a fish swimming at the other side of the boat.

'A trout! a trout!' cried she, starting up.

That moment, before Raoul could stretch out his arms to pull her to her seat again, Louise, sitting on the same bench, lost her balance, made one piteous effort to hold on by the boat's side, and then fell right into the lake.

CHAPTER XXIII.

ANGUISH.

SCARCELY had Louise sank under water, than Raoul, by a rapid, quiet movement, took off his jacket, slipped to the boat's edge, and letting himself drop gently into the water, vanished too. His mother did not utter a cry. Silently, her arms extended towards the three remaining children, she sat, looking like an embodied prayer, and gazing down into the spot where Louise had disappeared.

Once Louise rose to the surface, but Raoul was not near enough to catch her. He dived, and the half-bewildered boatman tried to guide the little skiff to where he was likely to reappear. At last there was a glimmer of white beneath the water, and the sound of arms beating it in rapid and regular motion. It was Raoul, who reached the boat's side, holding his cousin with one arm, and swimming with the other.

Madame de Bresse leaned forward, and with almost miraculous strength drew her niece into the boat, while Caroline did the same for Raoul. A minute more and both were safe.

Safe! when Louise had her eyes closed, her lips blue, her heart scarcely beating. Raoul seized an oar, and he and the boatman rowed ashore as fast as they could. Then Raoul, seemingly quite unconscious of fatigue, carried Louise; and Madame de Bresse, in spite of her mortal terror, felt a thrill of pride in seeing her young son so thoroughly a man.

'Go and change your clothes,' said she to

him, when he had laid Louise down upon the bed.

'And she, mamma?'

'She is alive,' was all the answer, for none other was possible. Further the aunt could say nothing, hope for nothing. Her sole prayer was that God might at least grant one moment of consciousness, in which the poor child, who had lived without thought of Him, might turn to Him in dying.

Raoul obeyed and went away. Anna, trembling violently, but always yielding to the force of a stronger will than her own, helped her aunt to undress Louise, to roll her in hot blankets, and do all else that is necessary for the recovery of the drowned. At length a slight motion was visible in the blue lips—a faint colour came into the cheeks—Louise opened her eyes.

'Aunt!' said she, in a voice so weak, that only Anna, who was leaning over her, heard it.

'She has spoken! she has recognised you!'

But already her eyes were shut again, and the insensibility returned.

The doctor was sent for.

'Only just in time,' said he. 'One minute more, and—I hope, Madame, you have pretty good health?' turning abruptly to Madame de Bresse.

'Yes; but why?'

'Because you will have a long nursing of your daughter; and you may thank God that she is not dead.'

Louise, opening her eyes, caught the last word.

'Dead! am I dead? am I going to die?' And lifting her arms above her head, she uttered piercing cries.

'Delirium,' said the doctor. 'But it's nothing, and quite inevitable. Only send these children away, madame. They must have been frightened enough already.'

Madame de Bresse told Anna and Caroline to go away, and then looked for Jeanne.

'Where is she?' she enquired of Caroline.

'Here, mamma,' whispered the frightened child.

Poor Jeanne was crouching in a corner, hiding from all eyes. Not a word had she spoken—scarcely had breathed, from the moment when Louise dropped under water. She thought she had killed her cousin.

'Go with the others; the doctor will not let you stay here,' said Madame de Bresse.

But Jeanne begged pitifully that, dead or alive, she might see Louise again.

'I have killed her,' said she, pressing tightly her mother's hand. 'And I will never forget her—never, never, never!'

The latter words became a cry of misery. Madame de Bresse took the poor child in her arms and carried her out of the room.

'No, you have not killed her; and I believe that she will live,' said the mother, with a certain severity which had a good effect in quieting

Jeanne. ' But if you cry like this, you will do me great harm. Be still, and thank God that your carelessness did not bring the fatal result that it might have done. Then go and see what has become of Raoul: tell him that Louise has spoken twice, and that the doctor is with her.'

When her mother had gone back to the sick-room, poor little Jeanne, unable to bear alone the reproaches of her conscience, and not daring to go near Louise's sisters, slipped out to Raoul's door; she knocked, but no answer came, so she entered.

Her brother was on his knees, praying so fervently that he had not heard Jeanne's knock. The little girl crept mutely up and knelt down also. Her brother was praying in a smothered voice for poor Louise—not her bodily life; for to him, young, strong, and full of hope, the moment his mother said, ' She is living,' he was no longer doubtful—but for the life of her soul, that higher and nobler existence which, both in this world and in the world to come, we call *salvation*; and he felt deeply how solemn ought to be to him as well as to his cousin the effect of this sudden nearness to death—the death so miraculously escaped.

Jeanne became quieter still; her brother's ardent faith made her long to pray also; she passed her arms round his neck and said softly—

'Brother, ask God to forgive me for rising up in the boat.'

Raoul started violently; he had thought himself alone. Then seeing his little sister all trembling and in tears, he remembered that it was through her fault that the accident had happened. Taking her in his arms, he prayed a few words more, and then rose. The child had ceased weeping, but clung to her brother closely still.

'Dear Raoul, Louise has spoken twice. Mamma sent me to tell you so. The doctor is in her room; we have been sent away. Do you think anyone will forgive me—anyone except God?' added she, in a low tone.

'Everybody will forgive you, poor little darling!' cried Raoul. 'Come, I will take you to Caroline and Anna.'

Jeanne shrank back terrified. 'Oh no, no! wait till Marie comes in.'

Raoul did not urge the matter, but placing his forlorn little sister in an armchair by the window, went out, hoping to meet the doctor. The old man was just quitting the room, holding in his hand Louise's beautiful chestnut hair, which had just been all cut off.

'Your mother told me to take this away,' said he, when Raoul had explained who he was. 'The poor child in her delirium looked at her hair in such distress. I believe we shall save her; she seems to have a good constitution; but it will be a hand to hand battle for life. Happily your mother seems a perfect sick-nurse. And who pulled the girl out of the lake; was it Ronteau, the boatman?'

'No, sir,' said Raoul, hesitating so much and blushing so deeply that the doctor guessed the truth at once.

'I declare, it was you! Well, I congratulate you. You must be stronger than you look, for it was no easy task, with all your clothes on.'

'God helped us,' said Raoul, in a whisper.

The doctor was touched. 'You are right, my lad. And neither will He forsake us now. Pray that He may aid the doctor, as He did the swimmer, in saving life.' And the honest man went back to his patient's chamber.

Madame de Bresse needed him much. Delirium had taken full possession of Louise. She fancied herself sometimes in the lake, drowning amidst its blue waters; sometimes at Paris, at a ball or party, impatient of her aunt's care, and criticising her young companions. She tried hard to spring out of bed, and uttered piercing cries, which did not surprise the doctor.

'The rheumatic fever may last long. She was very hot, and the lake water is very cold; but, please God, the delirium may pass away soon, and then we shall see our way. Have you got ice for her head, madame?'

'Yes,' and then Madame de Bresse enquired if the doctor had seen her son, and if he thought there was anything amiss with him.

'Not the least. He looks pale, which is not surprising; but he turns red enough when one speaks of all he has done for his sister.'

'Not his sister—his cousin. We are travelling together, my husband and I and our four children, my brother-in-law and his son and three daughters. She, there, is the eldest.'

'Motherless?' enquired the doctor, with a glance at Louise, who was a little quieter now.

'Her mother was my sister,' whispered Madame de Bresse; and for the first time her tears came. 'She has been dead two years. Her poor child there——'

'Will not follow the mother, I trust, for many a year to come. Now, madame, take a little rest if you can. I think my patient is going to sleep, and I will stay beside her.'

'And I will go to her sisters.'

But in quitting the room, she saw coming along the shore of the lake the five mountain-climbers, returning from their expedition, still unfatigued, laughing and chattering apparently in the highest spirits. Suddenly a waiter at the hotel saw them, and went and said something to them. Marie uttered a cry, and all of them darted forward to the hotel, at the door of which, hardly able to stand, the mother was waiting.

'She will live, Louis!' was all she said.

'Thank God!' and M. Rambert leaned against the balustrade. 'Where is she?'

'In my room.'

Without another syllable, they all three went

upstairs, M. de Bresse half carrying his wife. Her courage had held out while she had to bear up all alone; now that help had come, she broke down.

CHAPTER XXIV.

SICKNESS UNTO DEATH.

MARIE, without waiting to hear anything more, at the first word about the accident had darted off like an arrow, and rushing instinctively to her mother's room, was entering it abruptly, when the voice of Louise arrested her.

'Dead, dead!' the poor girl was muttering. 'Dead at the bottom of the lake. All alone, all alone!'

Marie had often nursed her sick poor—once a servant—and once her mother; but she had never seen anyone delirious before, and these pitiful accents smote her with terror. She opened the door nevertheless; but she did it softly and slowly, looking paler than the poor patient herself, who, half sitting up in bed, was extending imploring hands to the doctor.

He tried to calm her—' There, there child, it's nothing; you are safe in your bed;' but in vain, until Marie advanced. As soon as Louise saw her, she threw herself into her cousin's arms.

'Save me, Marie! Uncle wishes me not to be pulled out of the water; he thinks me too wicked to live; he won't let Raoul save me. Cruel Raoul, to let me go; I am sinking to the bottom! I am dying!'

Marie knew nothing of what had happened except by these incoherent words, but she answered at random—

'Raoul has not let you go, my darling,' said she gently, wrapping her arms round Louise. 'Go to bed, and do not be afraid; I will stay beside you, and God will take care of you. Hush, hush! Shall I sing to you?'

Without waiting reply, conquering her shaking voice, she began to sing a psalm of Marcello's. Her sweet pure voice acted like a charm on the sick girl: she grew quiet, lay watching Marie awhile, and then sinking back on her pillow, again fell asleep.

Her father, her aunt and uncle, were all at the door, but hearing Louise's shrill wandering talk sink gradually and the clear solemn tones of the psalm arise, they waited till it was finished, and the room was perfectly silent.

'She sleeps, but it will not be for long; the least movement is a torture to her.'

'Rheumatism?' asked M. de Bresse of his wife.

'Yes.' And she looked pitifully at her brother-in-law, who had sunk in a chair, his head between his hands.

'Still one more, slipping away from me!' muttered he.

'No, please God; no!' said Madame de Bresse. 'It might have been, but Raoul——'

'Was it Raoul? I thought it was the boatman who saved her.'

'Raoul left him no chance. Did you also think, Charles, that it was the boatman?'

'I did not understand it at all. I was sure that Raoul would jump in after her, but I did not think he had strength to hold her with one hand and swim with the other. Where is he now?'

'In his room, I suppose. I sent Jeanne to him that he might comfort her; she thought she had killed Louise.'

'Poor child!' said M. Rambert.

Louise now awaked from her brief sleep, and they entered her room. M. Rambert hurried forward, saw his daughter with all her hair cut off, and her head wrapped in compresses of ice, made an effort to come near her, and then, unable to bear the piteous sight, fled precipitately from the room. M. de Bresse had looked on from the door, but when he saw his brother-in-law hurry away in such distress, he followed. He could be of no use to Louise, so he thought it best to undertake the task of consoling her father.

It was a heavy task for everyone. Old Catherine could only take charge of Louise during the day, when she generally slept. Anna and Caroline did the same, sometimes giving place to Jeanne, whose despair Raoul had reasoned down, but not her remorse. In the delirium, which returned at intervals longer or shorter, and in the alternations of acute suffering and exhaustion, Marie was the only person who could soothe her cousin; though, in her right mind, Louise preferred the nursing of her aunt, who was more experienced, more strong, and perhaps more compassionate than Marie. She, herself such a brave girl, could not quite comprehend the groans of pain which burst from poor Louise whenever she was required to move. But when delirium came on, Marie's voice, Marie's songs, were all-powerful.

Consequently, all through the twenty-four hours Marie was constantly wanted, and constantly on foot. Madame de Bresse took the night-watching, nominally, but she had constantly to go and waken her daughter that she might come and soothe Louise, and give her a chance of sleep. In the day-time both went to bed; but Marie often begged to take a walk instead, assuring her mother that the fresh air was better for her than sleeping.

M. Rambert was quite overwhelmed. This tragic end of his pleasant holiday, his anxiety over his daughter, his regret at seeing his sister and niece worn out by cares which Anna's incompetence and Catherine's old age prevented them sharing, seemed to take away the little strength to battle with misfortune that his wife's death had left him. Day after day M. de Bresse used to find him leaning over the balcony which overhung the lake, with his eyes fixed gloomily upon it, making no effort either to bear or to shake off his sorrow.

'What would you do if you were in my place?' said he once to M. de Bresse, who, after Louise had had a bad night and seemed worse, was vainly attempting to encourage him.

'What would I do?' answered his brother-in-law, looking him gravely in the face; 'I think I would pray.'

'That is easier said than done.'

'Have you ever tried?'

M. Rambert went away. Did he try? Did he, for the first time in his life, ask God to comfort him, not only in his daughter's recovery, but in that bitter grief for the death of his wife which had dried up every well-spring of consolation in him, until the voice of the Comforter Himself came to be heard?

M. Rambert was not the only one whom M. de Bresse had to cheer. Anna, from the first, had given way to the strong conviction that her sister would linger awhile, and then die. All the sentimental notions in which she and her friend Mathilde had hugged themselves rose up; and it was with difficulty she could be persuaded to spend two hours a day in the sick-chamber. She felt it too much, she said—did they want to kill her as well as her sister?

M. de Bresse tried to rouse her out of this sentimental egotism, but Anna's exaggerated sensibility was as hard to fight against as her father's weakness and despair.

The nurses had a task more difficult still. Louise's pains, instead of diminishing, seemed to increase. Intolerable head-aches took the place of the delirium, and all medical skill sank powerless before the general depression of the system. Daily Madame de Bresse read to her niece a little, or said to her a verse or two out of the Psalms; but Louise appeared absorbed by her own sufferings. To her aunt she replied not a word, but when Marie spoke earnestly to her, she bade her hold her tongue.

'It is easy for you to speak—for me, I have only strength enough to suffer.'

So passed the days, dull and dreary. Already for three weeks Louise had been confined to her bed, and seemed no better. Her aunt was worn out with fatigue. One night, when she left the room to replace Marie in the night-watch, she fainted. When she came to herself, her husband said decidedly—

'I will take your place. If Louise wants anything I can call Catherine; but this night you must sleep.'

Madame de Bresse yielded. Louise was sleeping, and when her uncle took Marie's place at the foot of the bed, she did not notice the change of watcher. However, towards midnight she opened her eyes, and saw, in her aunt's place, the figure of a man, kneeling. At first she thought it was her father. But the posture surprised her. She tried to move, so as to see better. M. de Bresse heard her and came nearer.

'Is that you, uncle? Is aunt ill then? She gave me my soup at nine o'clock.'

'No, my child, she is not ill; only very tired, and I have sent her to bed. Do you want anything to drink? Shall I call Catherine?'

Louise wanted nothing, she said. 'Was it in nursing me that aunt has worn herself out so much?'

'Yes; but don't talk, or you will be tired too. Go to sleep.'

'I can't, and I am not in pain just now. Tell me, does aunt love me then so much? and I have not loved her at all. But I do love her now.' Louise spoke very earnestly, fixing her eyes on her uncle's face.

'I doubt not you love her, my child; you were a little mistaken with regard to her, that was all. Now go to sleep.'

'If you are praying, uncle, you may as well pray for me,' murmured Louise, already half in a doze, and went off to sleep again.

M. de Bresse, profoundly touched by this, the first sign of gratitude or feeling which the sick girl had shown, returned to his reading.

Louise passed an excellent night, and her uncle, telling his wife all that had passed, declared that he would no longer be excluded from the room, since his niece had chosen him for her confidant, and his presence had also exercised upon her such a soporific influence. In fact, let her pains be ever so sharp, whenever she heard her uncle's step, Louise henceforward would try to smile, and make an effort to hold out her hand.

One evening when her father was sitting beside

her, she heard M. de Bresse's step outside, and looked up.

'What are you thinking of, my dear?'

'I thought uncle was coming in,' said she, dropping back with an air of disappointment.

Her father sighed. He could quiet his natural jealousy, but it was hard for him to think that the first serious words which had touched the heart of his daughter should have come, not from himself. Nor was it to himself that she showed her gratitude.

M. de Bresse, quick-sighted in judging character, soon guessed this, and perceived that whenever M. Rambert visited Louise's room, he came away looking sadder than when he entered. One morning, walking on the shores of the lake, the two brothers-in-law, naturally so reserved both, kept mutual silence, until suddenly M. Rambert, seeing Raoul and Amédée row past merrily in their boat, said—

'Yes, it is to your son that I owe the life

of my daughter, and if she ever is worth anything it is to you and your wife that I shall owe that also.'

'Why not to her father, my dear Louis?'

'Me! Oh, I am good for nothing; it is only lately that I have found out I have a soul to be saved.'

'She has not yet found out that, poor child. Help us that she may soon.'

These words smote, like an arrow of light, into the father's heart. It seemed to him as if he, to whom she owed her earthly existence, *must* try to lead her somehow into that way of heaven which he dimly saw opening before him.

CHAPTER XXV.

DEATH PASSES BY.

AFTER some days Louise seemed to suffer a little less. She had better nights, and her patience—never much, poor child!—was not tested so severely. Sometimes she passed hours without stirring, absorbed in her own thoughts. She spoke little, and to Marie's surprise took small pleasure in being read to. But the mother, when she came in and found Marie, a volume of sermons in hand, seated by the sick-bed, and reading out resolutely in a loud tone to Louise, who, her head turned to the wall, listened out of mere civility, and without making any sense of the words—the wiser mother always closed the book, saying ' that the invalid was not strong enough yet for such solid food, and that she would gain more spiritual nourishment from five or six verses out of the Gospels or the Psalms than from all the sermons in the world.' Which saying a little scandalised Marie, who was fond of sermons.

M. Rambert preached none; but he came oftener into his daughter's room, sat beside her bed, talked to her affectionately, sometimes even read the Bible to her. Louise vaguely perceived the great change in her father; she felt an added tenderness in his very kiss, and on his sad face she fancied there came a new and wonderful serenity.

'Do you not think that papa is a little like uncle?' said she one day to Marie, who drew back surprised, nay, rather shocked, at the comparison. For M. de Bresse was tall, strongly built, his thick grizzled hair curled crisp round his head, and his black eyes, his firm and noble features, bore no resemblance whatever to the uncertain motions, absent looks, bowed figure, and bald crown of M. Rambert.

'I don't say they are alike in appearance,' continued Louise, impatient at her cousin's silence. 'Only there is something in their expression, something new; I can't explain it if you don't see it.'

Marie reflected a little. 'I perceive what you mean,'. replied she slowly—very slowly; for with Louise's words came a new hope: was this vague resemblance an indication that her uncle was beginning to see, in dim glimpses, the God whom her father had loved and served so long?

As the anxiety about the sick girl diminished, the impatience of the detained family increased. M. de Bresse took long walks with the three boys, shorter ones with Anna, Caroline and Jeanne, whenever they could be spared by

Louise, who was always asking for them. Mountain air, plenty of milk, and plenty of walking had done Caroline so much good that she declared Laura Marmet would not know her again when she returned to Paris.

'Ah! when shall we return to Paris?' sighed Anna.

She was tired of mountains, and the part she played as nurse to Louise was too small to occupy her time. Many times her aunt had tried to add to her responsibility, but she could neither lift her sister without hurting her, nor give her a drink without upsetting the glass, so that Madame de Bresse had to take the reins of government once more in her own hands, aided a little by Marie, and gradually by Caroline.

One day, the sky being cloudless, Louise had had her window half opened. She lay watching the sunbeams flicker on her sick-bed, where she had lain a whole month now, and listening to the stamping of the mules below.

'Aunt,' she asked, 'is anybody going on an expedition to-day?'

'Yes, my child: Anna, Marie, Caroline, and Jeanne, with your uncle and the boys, are going to drink milk at a mountain chalet, where the view is said to be superb.'

'Is papa going too?'

'No, he is tired.'

'Then, aunt,' and Louise half raised herself in her earnestness, 'why should not you go too? I wish you would. Papa will come to see me now and then, and Catherine will take care of me. Do go! I have made you lose all the pleasure of your tour.'

'But it was no fault of yours, my child, and I assure you I am more in my element in a sick-room than on a mule's back, clambering up a mountain.'

Here M. Rambert entered, and his daughter besought him to add his entreaties to hers.

'You will nurse me yourself meanwhile, won't you, papa?'

M. Rambert whispered to his sister-in-law, who hesitated still, 'Do go. It is the first time my child has ever asked me to take care of her.'

So the matter was decided. Amédée, with comical gestures of triumph, went off to fetch a fourth mule; and Marie, who disdained such humble equestrianism, marched off by her father's side.

Everybody was in good spirits. Louise must be better, since she herself sent all her nurses away; the weather was superb, and, for the first time these four weeks, Madame de Bresse was able to accompany her husband and children on one of the excursions which they so much enjoyed together. To the cloud of trouble which had hung over them succeeded that peaceful grateful feeling which made all the world look more beautiful, which indeed was hardly needed this exquisite day. Raoul, having in charge his mother's mule, walked by her side, so proud and happy that it made him silent.

'To-day, I can almost look on the lake without shuddering,' said Madame de Bresse, as they wound up the mountain-pass. 'But this journey might have cost us dear.'

'And now,' said Raoul in a low voice, 'it seems as if we were likely to thank God for it to the end of our days.'

'Yes,' said the mother; 'all the good that we vainly hoped and tried to do, in Paris and here, God has done in a moment.'

Raoul did not say what was in his mind, that God had used the agency of his own good parents to make Louise and her father understand the full meaning of that frightful warning. They continued to ascend, sometimes laughing merrily at those on foot, who often sat down exhausted on the roadside. Marie alone, who climbed mountains as seriously and energetically as she did everything else, never stopped except to look at the view, to collect flowers for Louise, or stones, at Caroline's entreaty, for Laura Marmet. A fresh trunk would become inevitable for these treasures; M. de Bresse, who had hitherto failed in losing any luggage by the way, lifted his hands and eyes in despair as he saw the saddle-bags swelling.

When these were enjoying their expedition, poor Louise also enjoyed her after-dinner toilette, alas! very simple now. Her hair, which was beginning to grow again, escaped in waves from under her cap; she tied it with a red ribbon, using no looking glass and spent her last remnant of vanity in decking herself a little for her father's visit.

'I must so manage that papa finds me good company,' said she, laughing, to Catherine, who was very near crying. 'You see, he has nobody but me to-day.'

Poor child! she would not have dressed herself with such care, could she have seen how pale and thin she was, and how, raised up on pillows, with her white lips drawn back, and scarcely hiding her teeth, she looked much more ill than when she was lying flat upon her bed. Her father was so painfully struck by it that he went to the window to hide his emotion.

'Yes; they are all away, papa,' said Louise, believing he was looking out after the excursionists. 'There is nothing left for you but to sit at the foot of my bed and be content with me all the afternoon.'

Her voice was so loving, her eyes so beseeching, that the poor father trembled with fear. Was his child becoming so sweet, so dear, just that she might be taken from him?

'I am quite strong to-day, papa,' Louise went on. 'Do you know, I ate this morning some beef-steak for my breakfast. And at three o'clock Catherine will bring me biscuits and cream. I hope I shall soon be well, and we may go home. You will all be getting tired of this place, and the boys ought to be back at college. Papa,' she added, after a pause, 'I have not yet seen Raoul.'

'Nor thanked him?'

'No, but I shall to-morrow. They will lift me to a sofa, and then fetch Raoul to me. I shall say to him—Ah! I don't know what to say.'

'Nor did I. Still, I think he understands my gratitude. Still, my child—if it were due to only Raoul—' added her father, hesitating.

'Yes, I know; God helped him,' murmured Louise softly. 'God did not wish me to die just then.'

'And now?'

'Now I know Him.'

'So do I.'

No more was said or asked, and the silence lasted long between the father and daughter.

Catherine entered with biscuits and a cup of cream. M. Rambert's thankful happiness affected even his judgment of things: as he watched his daughter eat he fancied her less thin, less feeble-looking. He began to hope that God, who had already been so merciful, would give her a longer span of life wherein to serve Him—wherein they two might serve Him together. Louise paused from time to time to look at her father, to show him how well she was eating, and to laugh at the mountain-climbers who were taking such a long expedition in search of cream. Not half so good, she said, as that which Catherine had brought her now.

The cream finished, Louise leant back, very tired.

'Papa, will you read to me?' said she at last.

Instinctively M. Rambert held out his hand for Louise's Bible, which had been her mother's. It gave him a pang at the heart, especially when he thought how often he had tried to wean his wife from it to worldly pleasures which she did not really care for. But the remembrance of her long patience, her unalterable sweetness, and her devotedness to himself, returned to him more vividly than ever, proving how deep in her heart lay that faith of which she had not dared to speak.

'What shall I read, Louise?'

'A psalm, papa; I can't tell what psalm it is, but it is the one which thanks God for all His benefits.'

When the merry troop of wanderers returned from their mountain, Madame de Bresse, opening the door of her niece's room, heard the concluding words of the psalm which begins, 'My soul, bless the Lord, and forget not all His benefits.' Her brother-in-law immediately closed the book, and departed, but as he passed her he pressed her hand.

CHAPTER XXVI.

A NEW CAREER.

THE travellers began now to plan their return. The difficulty was how to get Louise to a railway. Though it was a short journey, still the cold was already beginning to be felt on the mountains, bad enough for a person who shivered at the least breath of air. M. de Bresse proposed a *chaise-à-porteurs.*

'But who will carry Louise for fifteen leagues, my dear?' asked his wife.

'We will establish relays, the rest of us following on foot or in a carriage; and if the porters are tired out we will come to the rescue. What is the use of five men if their arms are good for nothing?'

'Imagine Louis harnessing himself to a *chaise-à-porteurs*! All very well for you, who have spent your life in doing things which make one's hair stand on end. But he!'

'He will do a great deal of which you would never suppose him capable. But perhaps that may not be needed. I'll go and see about things.'

Louise laughed at the idea of travelling in a *chaise-à-porteurs*. She had seen such a thing at the theatre, but deliberately to put oneself in a box and be carried by two men, she could not imagine it! When her uncle assured her he was in earnest about the matter she did not like it at all. It seemed such a ridiculous mode of transport for a young lady.

'Who will see you?' said Anna.

'It will be great fun, I think,' cried Caroline.

'No, it won't,' said Marie abruptly. 'But if it were more convenient to the rest, and would end the long imprisonment of the family in this place, I would not say a word, were I Louise, even if I had to be taken all the way to Geneva in a *chaise-à-porteurs*.'

Louise blushed; she had not yet learned to conquer herself in little things: twenty times a day she felt inclined to be selfish, impatient, exacting; but she was sorry for her faults; she fought against them; she asked God to help her to fight against them.

'Go for the *chaise-à-porteurs*,' said she, after an effort. 'You are right, Marie. What does it matter, even if one does look like an old woman of seventy?'

'All sick folk are like old folk, my dear,' said her uncle, smiling. 'And when one is not yet nineteen, one need not much trouble oneself about it.'

'Is one obliged to do so, even at seventy?'

said Madame de Bresse. 'Because I mean to be a very charming old woman.'

'You always were charming,' replied her husband, with one of those tender looks, all the sweeter because his reserve of character made them rather rare.

M. Rambert was anxious to return to Paris, so were Arthur and Amédée, whose classes re-commenced on October 7. Raoul ought to begin his law studies at once. But his mind was preoccupied with the sights of poverty and misery which he had met with in the winter, when he had taken his father's place as a sort of city missionary. He kept thinking of all the good to be done and the evil to be conquered among the poor. In his walks with his father, by the lake-shore and up the mountain-side, their conversation continually went back to the wretched houses and the still more wretched streets of the lowest quarters of Paris.

The *chaise-à-porteurs* arrived from a neighbouring town. Louise had already been up some days; she had walked about her room—nay, she had even got to the sitting-room. And she had accomplished her grand project: she had thanked Raoul for saving her life—if a clasp of the hand and a few stammering words could be called thanks. But Raoul remembered one thing she said,—

'You have given me time to learn to know God.'

'*He* gave it you,' was the answer; and they said no more.

Each new attempt at exertion that Louise made proved the more her extreme weakness. She was terrified at the journey, but from the day that Marie, with her usual blunt candour, had reminded her how inconveniently everybody was detained in Switzerland, Louise never once complained. She concealed her feebleness as much as she could, and carefully husbanded her small strength, to avoid her great dread, of falling ill again at Geneva, and so hindering the return to Paris. And when, on the eve of departure, the poor invalid, fatigued with all the confusion of preparation, felt inclined to cry, instead of tears, she prayed in her heart that she might not be ill until she reached home. Home was the summit of her ambition now.

At eight in the morning the porters were waiting in the vestibule of the hotel, as well as many of the people belonging to it, and staying at it, in order to bid adieu and a good journey to a family who had interested everybody so much. M. de Bresse went to these with his usual frank courtesy, thanked them warmly, but begged them to retire, as his niece was not strong enough to bear the excitement of so many strange faces. The good Swiss folk immediately vanished, and if the strangers had more curiosity, they were obliged to follow the same kindly example.

Presently M. de Bresse re-appeared, carrying

his niece in his arms. She was so muffled up in shawls, furs, and veils that she might well have been taken for an old woman. Beneath her wrappings her uncle felt her tremble. He placed her in her little equipage and called his wife to attend her. Louise was so pale that her aunt closed the door of the *chaise-à-porteurs* with much anxiety.

'She is very weak still, Louis,' said she.

Louise heard, and made a sign to her father. 'Do not be afraid for me,' she whispered: 'I said my prayers this morning.'

So they started.

The railway was reached at last, relays of porters being found at different villages on the road. Once, one of them being intoxicated, Raoul, Amédée, and Arthur took his place by turns, to the great trouble of Louise; but no harm ensued.

Geneva gained, it was decided to lessen the number of stages, and increase their length.

Besides, from thence M. Rambert, Arthur, and Amédée were obliged to separate from the rest, and go direct to Paris. Raoul wished to visit some places near Geneva, and it was good for Louise to repose a few days, and consult a medical friend of her uncle's in whom he had great confidence.

M. Rambert had at first made a few difficulties before consenting to leave his daughters; but business compelled him to go on, and his jealousy of his brother-in-law had now given place to the utmost affection and confidence. It seemed to him that M. de Bresse was never troubled or perplexed; and, as in one sense he who trusts in God never is over-anxious about anything, perhaps M. Rambert was right.

The parting, through so brief, was sad; and the new bond which had been formed between Louise and her father made it more painful still.

'I shall soon be quite well, dear papa,' said she, clinging to him. 'Then I will take such care of you that you will forgive all my faults.'

And as the father, perhaps not without cause, blamed himself a little for his daughter's errors, this forgiveness was easily promised.

The evening that M. Rambert departed, when the girls were gone to bed, and his mother was with Louise, Raoul entered his father's room, and asked him to take a walk with him along the shore of the lake.

For some time M. de Bresse had perceived that his son wished for a good long talk with him, about something which evidently occupied his mind; so he took Raoul's arm, and they strolled out together.

Suddenly Raoul asked, 'Father, do you wish me very much to enter the profession of the law?'

'Yes, I prefer it to most others; but if you have any other desire——'

'I have, and only one,' cried Raoul earnestly, 'and that is, to try to do a little good to the miserable poor of Paris. And if I have to work at law for two or three years, and then go away, how shall I ever be able to accomplish it? Oh father, if you had seen what I saw last winter!'

'I have seen it, my son. But I am not rich enough to maintain you now, and give you wherewithal to marry upon by-and-by, unless you enter some profession.'

Raoul blushed. 'Put me in an office as a salaried clerk; then mornings and evenings I shall be free.'

M. de Bresse regarded his son with astonishment. 'You a clerk? I thought you hated that shut-up monotonous life.'

'But I shall love it if it procures me the means to lead my other, my true life. What I want is time, and the possibility of remaining at Paris. I have thought of other plans, to be a clergyman, a missionary; but it seems to me that God calls me to labour for Him in Paris streets. One has no time to lose here below, father, and God will put His own words into my mouth.'

M. de Bresse, much touched, laid his hand on his boy's shoulder.

'I must talk with your mother. She may say, perhaps, that you can serve God everywhere, in the country as in the town.'

'I know that, but mamma is ignorant of all the misery there is in Paris. A whole army of missionaries is needed. I wish to be a humble soldier in that army, and it seems to me my post is in Paris. You, who know how much is to be done there, can explain this to my mother.'

'I will try,' said M. de Bresse as they went indoors.

Raoul had opened his heart to his father and was comforted. M. de Bresse also, moved by this youthful devotedness, began to consider how, without injuring his other children, he could help his eldest son to carry out the difficult career he had chosen.

But on telling all to his wife he found with surprise that the mother, while consenting that Raoul should renounce his destined career, objected to his being supplied with an income that would enable him to do without a profession.

'Let him make the sacrifice he wishes,' she said: 'it will fit him all the more to labour among the poor.'

'But it will give him less time to devote to them.'

'Less time, and more zeal. He is only nineteen yet; he requires method and discipline. Office hours will do him no harm. Besides, he will want money to distribute. Be content; you also will have your part in the sacrifice, which I believe was your chief inducement to it.'

M. de Bresse smiled. 'My chief inducement was to spare my poor Raoul a clerk's life, which will be insupportable to him.'

'Nothing will be insupportable to him if he believes he is doing the will of God.'

So said the mother, well knowing her boy, and the conversation stopped.

CHAPTER XXVII.

HOME AT LAST.

DURING two days, every time that Raoul met his mother he lifted his eyes, expecting her to speak, but she did not speak. Many times, however, she had spoken with her husband. He disliked asking for his son a Government clerkship.

'I have never yet asked such a thing of anyone,' said he.

The mother argued that it was a small favour, Raoul's aims being so moderate. Also, that if no place could be asked of Government, there were still banks open, and merchants' offices.

'Why not apply at Louis Rambert's? He would be delighted to get Raoul.'

This idea once started, Madame de Bresse avoided no longer the conversation with her son.

'Your father has told me your projects,' said she. 'I believe you are right, and I comprehend what claims Paris seems to have. You have been brought up there; you like the place.'

'Oh! mother, it is not that. I like no place so well as the little village we have just left, where we have been so happy.' (And Raoul blushed.) But it is at Paris that most work is found to be done, even by the weakest; and if my father can put me in a way just to earn my bread——'

'We thought of putting you with your uncle Louis.'

'I should prefer a common office. Uncle is

so good he would spare me all possible work, and yet I should not have my time after hours wholly to myself. But let it be as you will; you are only too good in letting me change my career.'

'Is it an office life you call your career?' said Madame de Bresse, with a tender look.

'No, mother, the other one,' replied Raoul softly, and both kept silence.

When her husband came back, the mother told him how Raoul evidently preferred a clerkship where his leisure hours would be all his own, and proposed that they should write to ask M. Rambert to procure him such a place.

'How people would laugh if they knew how and why our Raoul chose such a career as this!' said she.

'But, after all, I think I admire and esteem him more than if he had openly consecrated himself to the service of God. At his age, not even so high a motive could have made me accept such slavery. We must help him bravely to bear it.'

'Be at ease,' replied the mother. 'Take a walk with him, and set his mind at rest. He thinks his giving up the law goes to your heart.'

'It goes more to my heart to give up my good son to God,' said M. de Bresse as he went to rejoin Raoul and Marie, who were taking their last walk before leaving to-morrow.

The three others preferred walking through the streets of Geneva. Jeanne and Caroline were going to unite their finances in buying a brooch for Laura Marmet, whom Jeanne had often seen during the winter, and for whom she had conceived quite a passion. Catherine accompanied them, but the two little girls begged for Anna's help likewise.

'We don't understand the matter, you see; and, since Louise cannot come with us, you must, and give us your advice.'

'And see what a fine day it is,' pleaded

Caroline. 'We will walk on the quays, and look at the Rhone, which can plainly be distinguished —a dark stream through the blue waters of the lake. Only think: we leave to-morrow, and may never see these beautiful things again in all our lives.'

Anna was not sorry. She had admired mountains, rocks, and lakes, as she used to admire elegant dresses and lovely jewels—splendours which excited no longer the transports of poor Louise. But these latter had one advantage over the former: she had no trouble in going after them, while the admiration of nature was rather fatiguing. Anna thought her mountain adventures of this year would suffice her for the rest of her days.

Madame de Bresse proposed, since Anna was tired, that the brooches should be fetched and chosen here, by herself and Louise; at which the two little girls started in great delight to see about them. Anna took up a book and settled herself in an armchair by the window, saying she liked this best. But, secretly, a certain consciousness of the utter uselessness of her life made itself felt through all her laziness.

Louise, alone with her aunt, perceived that something was amiss. Louise was always quick-sighted, and illness gave her leisure, as well as unselfishness, so as to notice the cares of others. She soon saw that Madame de Bresse had something on her mind. Her dislike for her aunt had long since melted away into grateful affection. Long patience had borne its fruits: the tact which had thwarted none of her tastes whilst they remained innocent, the kindness which had been shown her in her money difficulties, had all been undermining Louise's resistance. She might have maintained it a little longer, but for the indefatigable devotion and tenderness with which she had been nursed since her accident. Then she succumbed. She recognized all her sins against her good aunt, and began to love her passionately.

But her affection was timid still, for she felt how little she had deserved kindness; and when her aunt leaned over her to arrange her invalid cap Louise put her arms round her neck and silently kissed her.

Madame de Bressé returned the kiss.

'We are happy and thankful to-day, my darling. Raoul has been opening up his plans for the future, and all we feel is, what an excellent son God has given us.'

'You knew that already,' said Louise. But when her aunt had explained all, she fell back on her pillows with a sigh of disappointment. 'All his life in an office!'

'All his life consecrated to the service of God,' replied the mother.

And Louise felt, not for the first time, how far behindhand she was in the devotedness of religious faith which animated her aunt, her uncle, Raoul, Marie. Still, her first step was taken, and she would walk on, feeble as she was, in the right road.

When, at seven P.M., the tourists came back, hungry, tired, and weary, Madame de Bresse saw that Marie had been taken into confidence, and was ready, heart and soul, to help her brother in his work. Only she did not like Raoul's earning his own livelihood; she would rather have had his parents maintain him.

'They will have to maintain me,' she complained, 'for I can earn nothing.'

'It is the lot of women,' said her father, laughing.

'Do you think mamma would have been the better for working for her bread?' asked Raoul, and so Marie's mouth was stopped.

Next day's journey was accomplished easily. The nearest approach to disaster was the brooch, which the little girls kept taking in and out of its box all day long to look at it, until Madame de Bresse declared it would surely be broken or lost before they reached Paris. But it also travelled in safety.

Louise's long illness and great weakness modified the family plans considerably. At first they spoke of spending the autumn at Bressuire; but Louise required constant medical care, and that was only attainable at Paris. Besides, in Raoul's new career, he needed support and strength; they could not leave him alone at once. And, as his wife said sometimes, M. de Bresse was almost jealous of his son, the missionary life was so completely his own vocation too. His Hebrew books remained unread, Chinese and Persian slumbered, while he went about with Raoul among the poor of Paris.

So they went back to their old lodgings in the Rue d'Anjou, but with circumstances totally changed. There Madame de Bresse had dreaded the opposition of her brother-in-law, the resistance of Louise, the coldness of the whole family—dreaded, and yet had met and conquered, all these things. And what unexpected comfort and joy came in their stead!

'And Anna?' suggested her husband, when Madame de Bresse was counting over all these blessings.

'Anna will follow the lead of the others, in good as in ill. Only I fear she will be disappointed if she expects her dear Mathilde to be her companion in all those occupations which Louise cares for no more.'

M. de Bresse smiled. 'Louise will never make a nun. Don't think it.'

'I neither think it nor desire it. I only wish her to live in the world, not as of the world, but as glorifying the name of our Master in the common life of every day. That is women's true vocation, my husband.'

'I know it, my dearest wife.'

And as he looked at her, there was no need to say that he knew one person at least by whom that vocation was constantly and faithfully fulfilled.

Spottiswoode & Co., Printers, New-street Square and Parliament Street.

www.ingramcontent.com/pod-product-compliance
Lightning Source LLC
Chambersburg PA
CBHW030322240426
43673CB00040B/1250